DR. MARK KAUFFMAN

KINGS ARISE

THE KINGMAKER ANOINTING

FOREWORD BY BISHOP GEORGE BENINATE

KINGS ARISE
The Kingmaker Anointing
By Dr. Mark Kauffman

ISBN: 978-1-7368361-7-0
LCCN: 2021918661

All Rights Reserved. No part of this publication may be produced or transmitted in any form or by any means without written permission of the author. The author guarantees all contents are original and do not infringe upon the legal rights of any other person or work.

Prepared for Publication By

PUBLISHING

MAKING YOUR BOOK A REALITY

Ceder Point, NC | 843-929-8768 | info@BandBpublishingLLC.com

Unless otherwise noted all scriptures are taken from The Holy Bible, King James Version.

Scriptures marked J.B. Phillips Translation are taken from The New Testament in Modern English by J.B Phillips copyright © 1960, 1972 J. B. Phillips. Administered by The Archbishops' Council of the Church of England. Used by Permission.

Scripture quotations marked NLT are taken from the Holy Bible, New Living Translation, copyright © 1996, 2004, 2015 by Tyndale House Foundation. Used by permission of Tyndale House Publishers, Inc., Carol Stream, Illinois 60188. All rights reserved.

To Contact the Author
DR. MARK KAUFFMAN
drmarkkauffman.org

CONTENTS

ACKNOWLEDGEMENTS 1
DEDICATION 3
FOREWORD 5
PREFACE 7
ENDORSEMENTS 11
INTRODUCTION 21
Kings Arise

CHAPTER 1 27
The Kingmaker Anointing

CHAPTER 2 49
The Royal Seed of Dominion

CHAPTER 3 63
The Priesthood Is Changing

CHAPTER 4 75
Transitional Glory

CHAPTER 5 85
The Caleb Generation

CHAPTER 6 95
The Kingdom of God

CHAPTER 7 109
The Presence Driven Life

CHAPTER 8.................................131
Restored Image

CHAPTER 9.................................161
A King's Excellence

CHAPTER 10................................175
True Worshipers

CHAPTER 11................................189
The Sons of God

CHAPTER 12................................217
The Foot Company

CHAPTER 13............................... 243
Leaping Into Destiny

Acknowledgements

To my lovely wife, Jill, who is the love of my life and my greatest inspiration as she labors with me in the Kingdom of God. Without her love, wisdom, knowledge, and companionship, this book would not have been penned and our ministry would not be what it is today.

I also want to pay tribute to my three sons: Christian Mark, Anthony, and Ryan, along with my three beautiful grandchildren, Alexandra, Mia Grace, and Michael. They are the joy of my life.

To Dr. William Hinn, who for the last 23 years, who has impacted and changed my life with his exemplary ministry and the revelatory insights into the Kingdom of God.

To Bishop George Beninate, whose prophetic insight and foresight has impacted my life and ministry for the last 30 years and continually encourages me to press toward the mark for the prize of the high call of God in Christ Jesus. Thank you for your kind words in the foreword of this book.

Special thanks to Theresa Burnworth for her excellent job editing this work.

To the amazing family at Jubilee Ministries International City Church in New Castle, Pennsylvania. They have given their lives in service to the Lord Jesus Christ and to the Kauffman family, thank you.

And most importantly, to the Holy Spirit, who has been my teacher.

Dedication

I dedicate this book to Dr. Don Nori Sr., who is a dear friend and companion in tribulation. He prompted me and inspired me to write this book, Kings Arise. A few months before he transitioned to Heaven, he sent me this text:

"Mark, when are you going to write that book? I'd like to see it. Our King has been bugging me for several weeks to ask you about a book. I'm generally reluctant to do that because I did it for so many years. I just wanted to make sure I was right in stirring that up in you. This morning, as I awoke, you were in front of me. I knew it was time!"

His life lives on through the many books he has written and the multitude of lives he impacted with his dynamic message.

I also dedicate this book to a dear friend of mine Pastor

Dominick Cestrone. Dominick has been a dear friend of mine for over 20 years. He has become a companion in tribulation and a friend that sticks closer than a brother! Together we walked through many perils of life and have built a covenant relationship with one another that is indissolvable. I salute you, Dominick!

Foreword

It is quite obvious that the Church has yet to fulfill Christ's final command to disciple all nations. The Gospel message of faith and hope has been ridiculed and debased, while the humanistic message of feel-goodism, diversity and inclusivism has ripped her children from her bosom. Her prophets are scorned, her authority usurped, her virtue ridiculed, her Lord and God mocked and defied. In the blasphemous name of "choice," sixty-five million unborn children have been torn from mother's wombs and murdered. Rather than striking fear in the hearts of those who oppose God and His Kingdom, the present day Church is perceived as an impotent and incompetent institution that has one foot in the grave and the other on a banana peel. But that is about to change!

In "Kings Arise," Dr. Mark Kaufman apostolicaly challenges every born-again spirit-filled believer to take up

Jesus' mantel of Kingship authority and Sonship inheritance and go and make disciples of ALL nations! He reminds all believers that the KING of kings and the LORD of lords has ordained Christians to be a people of purpose, power and authority. There is no doubt in my mind that "Kings Arise" will become one of the most influential books in ushering in the upcoming manifestation of the glory of God!

In "Kings Arise," the revelation of Jesus' absolute victory over sin, death and the grave will be made abundantly clear and the Church is a victorious conquering army of God. Every chapter of "Kings Arise" validates the fact that the Church is not only alive and well on planet earth, but she is being led by presence driven saints whose destiny is to tear-down demonic strongholds and assure the knowledge of the glory of the Lord covers the earth.

Dr. George R Beninate
Bishop of Christ the King Church International
General Overseer of Abundant Life Christian Training Center
Author of The Jesus Strategy, The Word of Agreement, Prophetic Worship, Thus Saith the Lord, The Age of Glory, Resurrection - Fact or Fiction, Showboat

Pittsburgh, PA USA & Phnom Penh, Cambodia

Preface

As I sit here to write the preface for this magnificent book entitled Kings Arise, I realize that this is unique. The author usually writes the preface. However, I was asked by my husband to write the preface and I am very honored to do so.

The church has operated efficiently in the priesthood mantle (prayer, praise, worship, intercession) and also in the prophetic. They are both powerful mantles. We get into His Presence as priests, and we hear His heartbeat. We then speak what we hear Him say with the prophetic mantle. But now it is time for a new mantle, a new anointing. Not only must we go into His glorious Presence, not only must we speak what He is saying, but now we must enforce it. We must take dominion over the worldly system and every principality and power that is not of our Father. There is a new (to us, not to the Lord!) anointing coming upon us–it is called the KINGLY anointing.

Every kingdom must have a king. Jesus Christ is our heavenly King, and King over all the heavens and all of the earth. However, in Revelation 19:16, He has on His vesture written King of kings and Lord of lords! He is King over other kings and Lord over other lords. The "other" meaning US! He has given us authority and dominion over the principalities, powers, rulers of this world and against spiritual wickedness in high places. (Ephesians 6:12) What a powerful anointing this is!

Ecclesiastes 8:4 says, "Where the word of a king is, there is power: and who may say unto him, What doest thou?"

As we begin to receive this call of kingship, not leaving the other things behind–we must continue as priests and prophets–our words have authority. Great authority. In the book of Daniel–once the king made a decree, it could not be revoked! This great authority has been passed to you and me through the blood of Jesus Christ as our inheritance.

This book, Kings Arise, is absolutely necessary to understand this kingly anointing. There are many prerequisites to becoming a king! It is not something to be taken lightly or loosely. A kingdom denotes government, authority, order, and rank. We must be willing in this great day of His power and come under His government and become the king that He is calling us to be. The worldly systems must come down and it will take a priest, prophet, and KING to dismantle that which is operating outside of the domain of our God.

"The kingdoms of this world are become the kingdoms of our Lord, and of his Christ; and He shall reign for ever and ever." Revelation 11:15

I believe this book will become a standard and a textbook for understanding this kingly anointing and mantle that is now coming to those who will accept what it takes to be a king. It is not for the faint of heart! But we have overcome the world and with great excitement and vehemency, take on the call to bring down the powers of darkness and create His kingdom in the earth!

I am honored to be a part of this great man of God's life, and I am privileged to take on this kingly call to advance the Kingdom of God in the earth! I hope you are too!

Dr. Jill Kauffman
M. Div., D. Div.

DR. MARK KAUFFMAN

Endorsements

Like most leaders, I read a lot of books to ensure my spiritual growth and leadership skills keep improving. Many books have sections that you can actually "skip over" while looking for the meat that really feeds your need at the moment. Not this one, Kings Arise is one continual blast from the Spirit of God to your spirit. You've heard the analogy of "drinking from a fire hose" but that doesn't tell the story here, Dr. Kauffman is an open flood gate of revelation regarding God's plan for His Church and His World, not in generalities but in detailed specifics that open your eyes to flash points of Truth. Kings Arise will give the believer a vision of hope for the future that is so necessary right now in our chaotic world and give us as speakers much food to feed the spiritually hungry we serve. After 42 years in full time ministry, I can't think of a book that has fueled my faith for total victory through Christ more than Kings Arise. I will share this book with all the ministers in our network and promote it to our congregations. THANK YOU Dr. Mark!!!

Dr. John Polis
President, Revival Fellowship International, Inc.

Kings Arise! is truly an apostolic and a prophetic proclamation! Mark Kauffman, an apostolic leader in the church and marketplace realms, gives honor to the King of kings as well as brings the biblical revelation of Kings Arise! His writing flows with the truths of scripture, revelation, and motivation for you to arise into your kingly mantle!

John P. Kelly
Founder and International Convening Apostle for International Coalition of Apostolic Leaders (ICAL)
Chairman of the Board for Lead Global 360
Founder and President of John P. Kelly Ministries, Inc.

Kings Arise is one of the most significant books written on the subject of leadership that we have today. Apostle Mark operates in his gifting to empower a generation of Kings both in the church and marketplace. This is a must read for those who are focused on reforming society. If your vision for the End Times consists of people hiding out in caves and praying that the Antichrist won't nab them, this book is definitely not for you. This book is for those who are called to rise up and reform the system, not run away from it.

Damian Williams
Founder of Leadership League. Executive Director of the River Network and advisor to leaders in the United Nations, Congress, NFL, and other marketplace and government spheres of influence

---

Kings Arise hits the mark. Full of purpose and challenges to enable us to build for the future. In this book Dr. Mark Kauffman appeals to us to move beyond cosmetic Christianity, into a life-giving relationship with Jesus Christ. He urges us to embody the biblical truths we hold dear while going after God with everything we have. Truly honored to write this endorsement for Kings Arise. Mark is someone who lives what he preaches. You will be drawn in by topics such as the Kingmaker Anointing, The Royal Seed of Dominion, and perhaps my favorite, Restored Image. This is a must read for those who desire to impact the day for God's glory!

Ruth Willard
Founder of KEY Fellowship Harrisburg, PA

This book, by my spiritual father, Dr. Mark Kauffman, is a living testimony of his daily life. Being part of many

Apostolic networks in the past 25 years, I have never seen the kingly anointing walked out in life like the example of Dr. Kauffman. This book is an invitation and impartation for YOU to reign as kings in life (Romans 5.17 AMPC). For years the Church has lived as Priests and Prophets, but God is taking us behind the veil with the revelation as sons of God to reign as kings in life. Creation is crying out for the sons (kings) to be manifested. This book provides the insight, guidance and living proof that the time is now to reign and rule the earth and for Kings to Arise!

Dr. Ed Turose
CEO, Focus Life Institute

Dr. Mark Kauffman has a brilliant presentation in his new book, Kings Arise, of the next move of God, the Kingdom Age, with unusual insight to scriptures that reveal the design and purpose, with practical applications he has already utilized. This is not a ponder some theological thesis, but rather a heart gripping revelation. I have been a first-hand witness of the fruit of his church loading over 700 vehicles with food every week that helps feed people within a 200-mile radius. Dr. Mark reveals the Kingdom Age while anchoring it deeper in the core values of Christianity. "Real power is measured by how much we love King Jesus." Dr. Mark unfolds revelation of the kingship of Jesus from His birth to His last days on earth confessing before Pilate, "I am a King." Expect to be provoke by his revelation to enter the fullness of your kingship for His glory on this earth. My best-selling book, And David Perceived He Was King, in six languages, is on identity. Dr. Mark's book brings added new light and revelation to our identity that he amazingly weaves throughout his book empowering us to new levels of purpose. Let's invite Jesus, our King, to arise through us as kings to bring the Kingdom of God from heaven to earth.

Dr. Dale L Mast
www.dalemast.org | Author: And David Perceived He Was King, Two Sons and a Father, The Throne of David, Shattering the Limitations of Pain

---

In his new book, Kings Arise, Dr. Kauffman identifies the new breed of leader God is raising up today. Those that will walk in the Kingly Mantle of dominion like Caleb taking out giants, taking back mountains, and transforming society with the culture of heaven. This book is filled with revelation explaining the process of maturing into the Kingly Anointing. I believe this book will help all of us attain to a higher level of service to our King Jesus.

Pastor Tony Flowers
Jubilee Ministries International

There have been many disparate writings and

discussions over the past twenty-plus years regarding various topics within the Great Commission command to build the Kingdom of God on Earth. Apostle Mark Kauffman has written with his tremendously revelational book Kings Arise the most comprehensive and facilitating work I have ever encountered for the purpose of affecting the Kingdom of God in this 21st Century. Every topic taught in Kings Arise is well explained and derived from an abundant and exacting use of Scripture. This is a concise, power-packed book that will greatly benefit all sons and daughters of our Lord Jesus Christ placed in all 7 spheres of society who earnestly desire to fulfill their God-given calling and assignment. Kings Arise will, I believe, become a timeless classic that will be strongly impactful and consulted again and again by many engaged in the great work of building and keeping God's Kingdom on Earth.

Glenn Thomas
Chairman and CEO of Regulus Energy LLC New Castle, PA

In every generation, God raises up brave men and women who hear His heart, and boldly, unapologetically proclaim the truth. They lead the way in revelation, proclamation, and transformation.

My good friend, Dr. Mark Kauffman is one such leader. For decades, he has been transitioning out of the old religious wine skin, into a wonderful, life-giving new wine skin. Gone are the dead traditions, churchy cliches, and fruitless activities.

Instead, he presents a blueprint for reformation. A clear and clarion call to a future, kingdom dynamic. This book is not for the faint of heart or for those looking to maintain the status quo. Instead, these words will challenge your foundations, your methods, and finally, your whole worldview. He speaks to the individual believer in a very personal way. He also addresses the mandate of local ministry. But maybe best of all, he paints the bigger picture of what God is doing globally... In every culture, and every nation.

If you are serious about fulfilling your destiny, if you have a passion to play a vital role in the Great Commission, if you are committed to taking up your cross and following Jesus, this book is a must read!

But... get ready for bold declarations, major paradigm shifts, and fresh revelation in the Word! All directed to bring change into your life. And don't say I didn't warn you!

Dennis Wiedrick

From the first sentence of this book, Dr. Mark Kauffman masterfully lays out how God is restoring the true identity of The Believers, while moving us from the Church Age to the Kingdom Age. Not only is this book written by revelation, you can feel the relationship and experience Dr. Kauffman has with the Lord flowing through on every page. "Kings Arise" will open you up to a re-visioning of how you see the church and how you do business; this book will shift your perception to a Heavenly view. This book is not just for leaders but a must read for every believer.

Lynette K. Dutton
CFO of The Dominion.TV Network

In this book, Dr. Mark Kauffman so brilliantly captures the heart of God concerning The Kingdom of God, The Church of Jesus Christ and the Believer's role in the grand scheme of Kingdom Things. Dr. Kauffman tackles many of the pressing issues today in the modern church; many that seem to have lost "The Old Paths" as she has attempted to become more relevant to society instead of revelational in relationship to God's ultimate intention for the earth. I have personally known Dr. Kauffman and his ministry for well over twenty years. This book not only speaks to us from a preacher's point of view; "KINGS ARISE" is written from the heart of a true apostolic father with the desire to mature the Body of Christ into the full stature of Christ, our King— and empower the Believer to once again reign in life. Buckle your seat-beat and prepare for turbulence— KINGS ARISE is going to take you past the storms of churchyness and into the Heavenly intention of, Thy Kingdom Come!

Dr. Joseph H. Dutton
Apostolic Overseer of Dominion Harvest Ministries, Inc And CEO of The Dominion.TV Network

---

It is a privilege to publish Dr. Kauffman's book, but even more so to read it. As I was editing, I was also making notes of the points that I wanted to go back and further study, such as moving to another level of excellence in my life, being more of a Mary than a Martha, and remembering that I am who He says I am. King's Arise gives Bible-based hope and that is exactly what our society needs right now... to understand that they were created for destiny...to be the David's, the Mary's, and the Caleb's of our generation! I believe that as people read this book, anxiety and depression will be lifted, passion created and/or reignited, and a desire to evangelize will emerge to bring the lost into the Kingdom. I know the Lord is going to move upon all that read this book as their eyes are opened and new revelation comes to their hearts.

Beth Mayer
B & B Publishing

DR. MARK KAUFFMAN

INTRODUCTION

Kings Arise

Presently, the Lord Jesus Christ is restoring the true identity of the church back to her. Falsified information has led the church into a mistaken identity, rendering her paralyzed, powerless, and impoverished. The method of falsified information goes as far back as the Garden of Eden when the devil told Eve, "If you eat this fruit, you will be like God." Adam and Eve were already like God, created in His likeness and image. These deceptive words from the enemy led Eve into an identity crisis. As a result, this identity theft led to the fall of all mankind. It's so important that you know who you are, what you have, where you came from, and why you are here if you're going to fulfill your purpose on the planet. Adam's wife Eve accepted her mistaken identity, and they lost everything. But the last Adam, Jesus' bride, the church, will recover her true identity and get everything back that was lost. In this present hour, Jesus is raising up a glorious church as His bride to recover her identity and all that was lost in the Garden.

A name is given to reveal your true identity. The children of Israel lived in bondage for 400 years because they lost their identity in Jehovah. But as soon as Moses led them out of Egypt, the Lord began to restore their identity by calling them a Kingdom of priests. Refusing to accept this newfound identity, they remained in the wilderness until they all died. The exceptions were Joshua and Caleb, who accepted their identity as kings and priests and were granted access into the Promised Land.

Churches are filled with people who have no life, no vision, no revelation, and no expectations other than Heaven. They lack dreams and aspirations for anything in this present life. Their only expectation is that of an escapist wanting to leave the planet instead of possessing a passion to change the planet. Many people have shunned the church, not because of Jesus, but because of His followers! Churches have become charismatic clinics for weak, passive, lukewarm people. Instead of empowering the saints to occupy, they give church therapy to baby Christians who never grow up.

But this is not the true apostolic church that the Lord is building and raising up in the 21st century. He is forming a people of purpose and destiny, a people filled with the Holy Ghost and power! This is a presence driven people that chase God with their whole spirit, soul, and body. They will be known as a righteous, royal priesthood of kings and priests who change society, reform culture, transform cities, and invade every sphere of their world with the Kingdom of Heaven! As priests, they are worshipers and as kings they are warriors. These worshiping warriors live by Heaven's mandate to have dominion. Their dominion flows out of their identity in Christ.

They are the sons of God who are a military might, delivering creation from its present bondage. As change agents sent by God, they are on assignment to start a God Revolution in this present world. This new, chosen generation is on fire for Jesus Christ and His Kingdom. They are a radical remnant, invading and disrupting their world by bringing days of Heaven upon the earth!

They are the most powerful army that hell has ever faced, known as the Foot Company, feared by demons and devils like no other generation. The powers of darkness are threatened by the very rising of this militant might, knowing that they are anointed to bring all their enemies under their feet!

This glorious church that Jesus is building is manifesting Christ's healing power, delivering power, saving power, miracle-working power, and life transforming power! Their love, authority, and power manifest with signs, wonders, and creative miracles. They have been given the power to create wealth to establish the plans and purposes of God in their present world.

So prophetic are the creative words of this new breed of believers, that they impregnate barren places. With their words, they reshape, rebuild, and revive that which is bound, broken, and bruised. The Spirit of the Lord rests upon them as they are called and chosen to rebuild the ancient ruins, raise up new cities destroyed long ago, and revive the devastations of many generations.

Angels are assigned to minister, protect, and co-labor with this royal priesthood of kings and priests! As priests, they take charge of environments and as kings they rule and reign in the earth! Their desperate thirst, passion, and pursuit for King Jesus set them apart and make them a lethal weapon in the hands of God! Their addiction to King Jesus grants them a mantle of zeal, taking vengeance and prevailing over the powers of darkness.

They are a mighty, overcoming army of reformers, who are the sent ones of God to change their world! As Heaven's Bridal Company, they will establish the Presence of God for generations to come! This is the true church that Jesus is building today, and the gates of hell cannot prevail against this glorious, end-time apostolic church. This radical remnant of overcomers is the GREATEST GENERATION THAT EVER LIVED!

Now is the time, the set time, for THE KINGS TO ARISE!!

DR. MARK KAUFFMAN

Chapter 1

The Kingmaker Anointing

A new day has dawned upon the church of Jesus Christ, and we are living in an epic moment in the church's history. We are currently amid a third reformation where the Lord is restoring His Kingdom and the kingly anointing to the body of Christ. The restoration of our identification as kings restores our dominion and authority over all our enemies, gives us power to create wealth, empowers us to rebuild wasted cities, and equips us to influence and occupy the seven mountains of society. The seven mountains include religion, family, education, arts and entertainment, media, government, and business. To influence these spheres, we need more than our priestly anointing; it requires a kingly anointing.

Whom the heaven must receive until the times of restitution of all things, which God hath spoken by the mouth of all his holy prophets since the world began. - Acts 3:21

For the Son of man is come to seek and to save that which was lost. - Luke 19:10

As a young boy, I grew up hearing my preacher say that Jesus came to save THEM that were lost. My preacher misquoted this Scripture. This verse tells us the Son of Man is come to seek and save THAT which was lost, not just THEM that were lost. Yes, He came to restore THEM that were lost, but it's much bigger than just THEM who were lost. He also came to restore THAT which was lost in the Garden of Eden.

And God said, Let us make man in our image, after our likeness: and let them have dominion over the fish of the sea, and over the fowl of the air, and over the cattle, and over all the earth, and over every creeping thing that creepeth upon the earth. - Genesis 1:26

Jesus came to restore our true image in God and our royal dominion back into the earth. What the first Adam lost, the last Adam, Jesus Christ, recovered. This passage of Luke 19:10 is the Son of God's mission statement. Once our true identity in Christ is restored, then our dominion in Christ is restored. The Bible is very simple: it is about a King, His Kingdom, and His Kingdom citizens.

Let's look at how, over the last 500 years, the Lord Jesus Christ has restored our priestly anointing, prophetic anointing, and is now restoring our kingly anointing back to His church. As the church of Jesus Christ emerged from the Dark Ages, God raised up a man by the name of Martin Luther, who led the First Reformation of the church. This took place in the early 1500s, known as the Protestant Reformation. Luther was ordained to the priesthood in 1507. A German professor of theology, author, composer, and a monk, Luther had a direct revelation from the Lord that embodied three fundamental beliefs. The first was salvation by faith alone, the second established the Bible as the only authority, and the third identified the priesthood of all believers. His revelation announced that every born again saint could have an intimate, personal relationship with Jesus Christ. They could worship the Lord and hear God for themselves. It was during this First Reformation that the Lord restored our priestly anointing. Over the next 400 years, the principles of holiness, baptism of water by immersion, the power of the blood of Jesus and the sanctification through the Holy Spirit were also restored to the church of Jesus Christ.

The Second Reformation began in the early 1900s, and one leader was William J. Seymour, an African American preacher. The Asuza Street revival began April 9, 1906. Seymour and seven other men were waiting on God on Bonnie Brae Street when suddenly, as if they were hit by a lightning bolt, these seven men were knocked off their chairs onto the floor and began to speak in tongues and praise the Lord. Word quickly spread around the city, and crowds gathered within a few days. The testimony of those who attended the Asuza Revival was, "I'm saved, sanctified, and filled with the Holy Ghost." This was the beginning of the Pentecostal movement that would last for one hundred years. The prophetic anointing was now being restored to the church, whereby all God's people could prophesy and become a prophetic people. This would include the Holy Ghost baptism, restoring of the 9 gifts of the Spirit, praise and worship, the Word of faith, healing of the mind and body, and the restoration of five-fold leaders.

And he gave some apostles; and some prophets; and some evangelists; and some, pastors and teachers; For the perfecting of the saints, for the work of the ministry, for the edifying of the body of Christ. - Ephesians 4:11-12

This was also the beginning of the prophetic movement. Throughout the 1900s, as the Lord restored the prophetic anointing back to the body of Christ, they could walk as a prophetic generation.

Have not I written to thee excellent things in counsels and knowledge? - Proverbs 22:20

As we see in this verse, the Lord speaks to us in more

excellent ways. The word excellent is rendered in the Hebrew as triplicates or threefold ways. Examples include:

- The Father, the Son and the Holy Ghost
- Spirit, soul, and body
- Faith, hope, and charity
- He is the Way, the Truth, and the Life
- His ministry as Prophet, Priest, and King
- Outer Court, Holy Place, and Most Holy Place
- Thine is the Kingdom, the power, and the glory

These are just a few examples of how God operates in threefold expressions. The threefold excellence of God encompasses everything that God does. God is a God of excellence, and we see this principle throughout the Old and New Testaments. Jesus came to earth as a priest, a prophet and the King and as He is, so are we in this world. The God of triplicates is now, in this glorious time in the history of the church, restoring our kingly mantle.

JESUS CAME TO EARTH AS A PRIEST, A PROPHET AND THE KING AND AS HE IS, SO ARE WE IN THIS WORLD.

While writing this book, in this present hour, the church is coming into a third and Final Reformation. This reformation is restoring the kingship anointing to the church of Jesus Christ. During this Kingdom season, the Lord is revealing our identity as the sons of God. In this new season, we will see the Kingdom of God manifested in and through the church. We will experience the glory of God like no other generation. The saints will be carriers of the presence of God, manifesting His presence for all the world to see. We will disciple nations and move in a corporate anointing; the anointing poured out on all of us is far greater than the anointing that rests on any single person. Our corporate anointing will be greater than any individual anointing. As one puts 1,000 to flight, just two of us can put 10,000 to flight. Together, we are more contagious than infectious diseases! This Third Reformation of the kingly anointing: restores dominion over all our enemies, empowers us to repair cities in waste, raises up former desolations, allows us to walk in the supernatural power of the Holy Ghost, helps us to obtain power to create wealth, and equips and anoints us to influence the seven mountains of our society with the culture of Heaven. The Third and Final Reformation restores the apostolic movement, marketplace ministers, wealth creation, the rise of the sons of God, and the rule and reign of Christ in the earth through His church, the bride of Christ. This reformation is not only for a handful of ministers, but it's a reformation that equips and empowers all the saints to bring days of Heaven upon the earth.

That your days may be multiplied, and the days of your

children, in the land which the Lord sware unto your fathers to give them, as the days of heaven upon the earth. - Deuteronomy 11:21

This is what we are calling THE ALL SAINTS MOVEMENT! My very good friend Bishop George Beninate, in his new book, calls this next season in God, "THE AGE OF GLORY."

Presently, the church of Jesus Christ is leaving one season and preparing for the next. I was inspired to write this book by the Holy Spirit with the purpose and intent to bring a clear understanding to the reader about what this next season in God looks like. I don't know all that God will do in this season, for we know in part and we only see in part. Therefore, I'm sharing the part the Holy Ghost has shared with me. The church is presently moving from the Church age into the Kingdom age, embodied well in Bishop Beninate's description, "THE AGE OF GLORY." This doesn't mean that we are leaving the church, just leaving the church as we have known it. The church of Jesus Christ is not an event, and it is not a building in which we meet once or twice a week for encouragement and therapy. The church of Jesus Christ is a military might of kings and priests, a chosen generation, a called-out platoon, the sons of God sent as ambassadors from Heaven into this present world to reform, reclaim, renew, rebuild, revive, restore, and reshape the world in which we live.

The Greek word used for church in the New Testament is ekklesia, meaning called-out ones. I grew up believing the church was a place where we met every Sunday morning to sing songs, hear a Word from God and have fellowship after. Thayer's Lexicon describes ekklesia as "an assembly of the people convened at a public place for counsel to deliberate." The church of Jesus Christ is the governing body of Christ in the earth to establish and demonstrate the Kingdom of God. They are called out and chosen by God to steward His Kingdom on the earth.

But ye are come unto mount Sion, and unto the city of the living God, the heavenly Jerusalem, and to an innumerable company of angels, To the general assembly and church of the firstborn, which are written in heaven, and to God the Judge of all, and to the spirits of just men made perfect. - Hebrews 12:22-23

The church of Jesus Christ has been granted authority to govern all aspects of life. The Lord calls us His general assembly.

Thou shalt also decree a thing, and it shall be established unto thee: and the light shall shine upon thy ways. - Job 22:28

Every week the church is called to gather as the general assembly and pass legislation by releasing the decrees of Heaven over social, political, and community issues.

Verily I say unto you, Whatsoever ye shall bind on earth

shall be bound in heaven: and whatsoever ye shall loose on earth shall be loosed in heaven. - Matthew 18:18

Through the keys of the Kingdom we have been given legal authority to bind and to loose; these are legal terms. Therefore, what we permit shall be permitted and what we don't permit will not be permitted — this is the true authority of the church. We must not permit sickness, poverty, witchcraft, prostitution, drug lording, or crime to be in our cities. We must rise up and use the keys of the Kingdom to execute judgment against the powers of darkness. Jesus took His apostles to the darkest place on earth (Caesarea Phillipi) and gave them the legal authority to open the Heavens and shut down hell. When we gather, we pray God's Kingdom come and His will be done in earth as it is in Heaven. Therefore, we exercise our covenant rights and authority as kings to bring God's Kingdom into full manifestation in the earth.

Now then we are ambassadors for Christ, as though God beseeched you by us: we pray you in Christ's stead, be ye reconciled to God. - 2 Corinthians 5:20

We are sent here as ambassadors of Christ, representing the Kingdom of Heaven upon the earth. Ekklesia also means that parliament is in seat. Just like Great Britain, their parliament is comprised of a house of lords who represent their country. Likewise, the Kingdom of God has a house of lords as well. Jesus is Lord of lords, and we represent Heaven upon the earth. A lord has delegated authority.

Jesus said that His church was to be a house of prayer to all nations. As we gather, we pray and make decrees whereby we pass Kingdom laws and make righteous judgments. This is the true church of Jesus Christ that He is raising up in this present hour. The church is not to separate themselves from the world but to invade and change it. Jesus said, "Occupy till I come."

> *O sing unto the Lord a new song; for he hath done marvellous things: his right hand, and his holy arm, hath gotten him the victory. - Psalm 98:1*

Jesus is King of kings and Lord of lords. As kings and lords of His Kingdom, we operate as the governmental arm of Heaven, charged to proclaim, impart, and demonstrate the Kingdom of God in the earth. As you can see, the church does more than pour oil into wounds, encourage one another and have fellowship together. Under His Lordship, we come together to pass legislation that will change our territory and advance the Kingdom of Heaven upon the earth.

> *For if by one man's offence death reigned by one; much more they which receive abundance of grace and of the gift of righteousness shall reign in life by one, Jesus Christ. - Romans 5:17*

We come to equip and impact the saints to empower and prepare them to change the world to look like Heaven. The Kingdom church is not a maintenance center to maintain your salvation until Jesus comes, but it's an empowerment center to train the saints to reign in this life.

The elder unto the elect lady and her children, whom I love in the truth; and not I only, but also all they that have known the truth; For the truth's sake, which dwelleth in us, and shall be with us for ever. - 2 John verses 1 and 2

With such profound imagery, John calls the church the elect lady. Elect in the Greek means chosen and favorite. The church of Jesus Christ is chosen in Him from the foundation of the world sent here into the planet to influence it as salt and light. Her mandate is "Thy Kingdom come, Thy will be done in earth as it is in Heaven."

Thus, we have been given a mandate to see His Kingdom come and His will be done in earth as it is in Heaven.

O sing unto the Lord a new song; for he hath done marvellous things: his right hand, and his holy arm, hath gotten him the victory. - Psalms 98:1

The Lord hath made bare his holy arm in the eyes of all the nations; and all the ends of the earth shall see the salvation of our God. - Isaiah 52:10

The church of Jesus Christ is His holy arm, the extension of King Jesus in the earth; we are the governmental arm of Heaven. Jesus didn't come to bring a religion, but to bring a government called the Kingdom of Heaven. The church's mission is to recover the earth and bring it under the Lordship of King Jesus. We are called to transform the planet to look just like Heaven. We are charged to proclaim, impart, and demonstrate the Kingdom of God in all the earth. We are called to make Him King and Lord over all the earth! That's the church of Jesus Christ. We are sent ones, called to go into the darkest places on earth and transform them to look like Heaven.

Ask of me, and I shall give thee the heathen for thine inheritance, and the uttermost parts of the earth for thy possession. - Psalms 2:8

In this new season, we are promised that God will give us the heathen for our inheritance. The prostitute that you drive by every day on the way home from work is your inheritance. The drug addict standing on the street corner selling drugs is your inheritance, and those orphaned, homeless children are the inheritance of the church of Jesus Christ. We will go into greater depth of who the church is in the earth in a following chapter.

For the last 2000 years, we have been living in the Church Age. But presently, a new season is here called the Kingdom Age. Therefore, we are in a position that I call "A PLACE IN BETWEEN." We are the generation standing in the gap between two ages of time. I will clarify what this place called "In Between" looks like in a future chapter. We presently stand in a post-charismatic, Pentecostal season that is characterized as the Apostolic, father-son, Kingdom

Age. While the past season that we have just come out of was seasonal, the Kingdom Age we are coming into is perpetual and without end.

Of the increase of his government and peace there shall be no end, upon the throne of David, and upon his kingdom, to order it, and to establish it with judgment and with justice from henceforth even for ever. The zeal of the Lord of hosts will perform this. - Isaiah 9:7

The Kingdom of God is an ever-increasing Kingdom. Those who live in Christ's Kingdom can expect God to increase them more and more. Everything about this season is about the increase of favor, authority, power, signs and wonders, wealth, harvest, glory, presence, anointing and influence in the sphere that the Lord has called us to.

The Lord shall increase you more and more, you and your children. - Psalms 115:14

In the previous season, the Lord prepared a company of Samuels, who have been anointed and called as KINGMAKERS to raise up kings for the Kingdom Age. Samuel was a prophet of his day when there were no kings. Samuel was also a judge. The Old Testament judges were a prefigure of New Testament apostles. Therefore, he operated as an apostle and a prophet. Samuel represents the prophetic, charismatic, Pentecostal movement of the last season. The Lord called Samuel to make kings, for he had been given a kingmaker anointing. It was Samuel who anointed David as a king. There are Samuels present in this day from the prophetic era who have been called and anointed to raise up kings after the order of King David.

> *Then all the elders of Israel gathered themselves together, and came to Samuel unto Ramah, and said unto him, Behold, thou art old, and thy sons walk not in thy ways: now make us a king to judge us like all the nations. But the thing displeased Samuel when they said, Give us a king to judge us. And Samuel prayed unto the Lord. - 1 Samuel 8:4-6*

The elders of Israel made Saul a king using a vial of oil (representing a man-made anointing). Religion cannot make kings. This requires the anointing of mature apostles, prophets, and other five-fold leaders. Through Samuel as an apostolic, prophetic figure, God made David king by anointing him with oil from a ram's horn (representing a God-made anointing). David was chosen by God and not by men. If you're reading this book and have made it this far, you too have been chosen by God to be part of a company of kings in the earth that will rule and reign with Christ.

> *So the last shall be first, and the first last: for many be called, but few chosen. - Matthew 20:16*

I like to explain this Scripture in this way: many are called, but few choose to respond to the call. My desire for every one of you reading this book is that you would not only hear the call, but you would also respond to the call to be a king in Christ's Kingdom.

Many apostles and prophets of the prophetic era possess a kingmaker anointing. The emerging kings in this new order of ministry will look like King David.

> *In that day shall the Lord defend the inhabitants of Jerusalem; and he that is feeble among them at that day shall be as David; and the house of David shall be as God, as the angel of the Lord before them. - Zechariah 12:8.*

This is a powerful verse pointing to a Davidic generation, comparing even the most feeble among them to be like David! As they will rise with a kingly anointing, they will subdue all their enemies and take out our present-day giants, as David did in his day. We are now ushering in the kingship of believers and the dominion of the church. This company of Samuels that God has raised up from the last season as kingmakers will pour oil on the Davids of today and prepare them for their kingly anointing.

> *Then Samuel took the horn of oil, and anointed him in the midst of his brethren: and the Spirit of the Lord came upon David from that day forward. So Samuel rose up, and went to Ramah. - 1 Samuel 16:13*

From the moment that Samuel poured oil on David's head, David began to walk in his identity as a king from that day forward. If you don't have a Samuel in your life now, pray that God will lead you to one who can father you, mentor you, anoint you, and lead you into your identity as a royal king.

> *So the Philistines were subdued, and they came no more into the coast of Israel: and the hand of the Lord was against the Philistines all the days of Samuel. - 1 Samuel 7:13*

This passage of Scripture tells us the hand of the Lord was against the enemies of Samuel all the days of his life. The kingmaker anointing brings a restraining order against evil. Samuel poured the oil that was upon his life into David's life, empowering David to bring forth a restraining order against all the enemies of his day as well. One man's mantle covered an entire nation and brought restraint to evil. It is the hand of the Lord that accomplishes this in our day. We know God doesn't have a literal hand because He is a Spirit, but this is symbolic (the Lord is the great symbolist). The hand represents five-fold ministry restored into the earth. When cities do not have five-fold ministries, they suffer and struggle to overcome their enemies. The kings that are emerging in the earth today are called, anointed, and appointed to bring restraining orders against crime, violence, drugs, witchcraft, corruptions, perversions, and religious spirits. As these kings arise, their mantles will cover entire cities, heal the land, and bring a restraint against evil.

Several years ago, several psychic centers opened in our city. We declared that was not permissible under our watch and the psychic centers would not be permitted to influence the citizens of our community. We were prompted by the Lord to go to these three psychic centers to gather pamphlets of information about their business. We brought them back to the church parking lot, prayed over them, and burnt them all. Then we made decrees of restraining orders over those businesses, proclaiming that they did not have permission to operate in our city. After we placed a restraining order against these centers, within a few months, they closed and left the city.

On another occasion, we had a radical terrorist group that wanted to move into our city. In 50 other cities in the United States, this group had successfully moved in and influenced the culture of these places. I had a visit from a FBI agent that warned me of this dangerous group and how my life could be in danger if we deprived them of coming into our city. But we know that no weapon formed against us shall prosper and that nothing, by any means, shall hurt us. We knew the Lord was with us and that He had called us to this assignment. The future of our city was at stake. We would not permit our city to be held hostage by a terrorist group. As apostolic and prophetic gatekeepers of our city, we rose to the challenge and through daily prayer with our intercessory team and our kingly decrees; we created a movement with government officials and the citizens of our community that kept the terrorists from overtaking our city. Upon their departure from our city, one leader paid me a visit to tell me in his own words "we successfully came into other cities, but we weren't able to do it in yours, therefore we are leaving." This was a tremendous success in the history of our city as we fulfilled the Scripture given to Abraham and his seed that we would possess the gates of our enemies! We protected the gates of our city by releasing a restraining order as kings in the earth and brought glory to God and His Kingdom.

The church has always thrived in the middle of a dark, pagan society.

> *Arise, shine; for thy light is come, and the glory of the Lord is risen upon thee. For, behold, the darkness shall cover the earth, and gross darkness the people: but the Lord shall arise upon thee, and his glory shall be seen upon thee. - Isaiah 60:1,2*

Prior to the Covid-19 pandemic, the church was declaring the authority that they had in Christ. Then when Covid hit, everybody went into hiding. If the world is scared and the church is scared,. where is our hope? The emerging kings are mantled for the challenge, for we have come to the Kingdom for such a time as this. Instead of resembling many believers who are looking to evacuate the planet and retreat, we are like David, who ran after Goliath. We are ready to run to take out the giants of our day and to run to a groaning creation. We have been commissioned to transform our present culture. The present war we are in is a war for the culture. It's not about growing our churches, but warring to capture the culture of society and transform it to look like Heaven. The moment is dripping with opportunity!

> *And when he had removed him, he raised up unto them David to be their king; to whom also he gave their testimony, and said, I have found David the son of Jesse, a man after mine own heart, which shall fulfil all my will. - Acts 13:22*

The emerging kings are like David—men and women after God's own heart, or may I say it this way, they are men and women that are after God. They will know the need of God, the passion of God, the purpose of God, the interests of God, the plan and mind of God for the season we are now in.

> *And such as do wickedly against the covenant shall he corrupt by flatteries: but the people that know their God shall be strong, and do exploits. - Daniel 11:32.*

Real power is measured by how much we love King Jesus. The most militant thing that you and I can do is to know Jesus. To know Him in Scripture means to be intimate with Him. Knowing in this verse comes before doing. We cannot do the great exploits that we have been sent into the earth to do without an intimate relationship with King Jesus. We are called to be both the bride of Christ and the sons of God in the earth. As the bride of Christ, we have a deep, intimate relationship with our Heavenly bridegroom King Jesus and as the sons of God, we demonstrate Him in all the earth. It should be our desire to be like the five wise virgins in Matthew 26, who, at the midnight hour, a time of transitioning from one day to the next, were prepared by trimming their lamps and filling them with oil. These five wise virgins had an intimate relationship with the bridegroom, but the five foolish were told by the bridegroom, "Verily I say unto you, I know you not." Failing to cultivate an intimate relationship with the bridegroom, the five foolish virgins received a closed door, keeping them out of the next season. Everyone must pay the price and go through our own process to prepare for the anointing oil. The context of this anointing oil is a spirit of readiness. This anointing is not awarded to anyone because you're saved. It must be purchased and gained by preparation, and it must be pursued by a presence driven life. Elisha pursued Elijah for 20 years before he received the double portion anointing. We live in a generation that wants everything instantly. Our purpose is to be intimate with the Lord and our destiny is to manifest Him. If there is no intimacy, there will be no oil; we must be a people of prayer, meditation of the Word, worship, harbor a willingness to go to through the process, cultivate a disciplined life, and keep connected to the corporate body of Jesus Christ. Preparation is never wasted in God's Kingdom. We cannot be like the five foolish virgins who wanted to live off of the five wise virgins' anointing; we must get our own. It is in your midnight seasons where your anointing is determined. When you are in a midnight season, when a crisis hits you, you will need to have some oil on you. We are now in oil buying time and overlapping lamp trimming time. The foolish virgins had gifting, talent, and intellect, but they saw no need for oil. In this new season, gifts and talents are not enough. The wise virgins purchased oil in the downtime while the bridegroom delayed. During delays, setbacks and at the times when God seems to procrastinate, during those mundane and boring hours is when we must trim our lamps and have a spirit of readiness. To get this fresh, kingly oil that Heaven is offering, you will need to be desperate. Divine insanity gets the anointing! The key of intimacy will open up doors that no man can shut that lead us into this new season which God has prepared for us. These emerging kings will know and manifest King Jesus like no other generation!

DR. MARK KAUFFMAN

CHAPTER 2

The Royal Seed of Dominion

And from Jesus Christ, who is the faithful witness, and the first begotten of the dead, and the prince of the kings of the earth. Unto him that loved us, and washed us from our sins in his own blood, and hath made us kings and priests unto God and his Father; to him be glory and dominion for ever and ever. Amen.- Revelation 1:5-6

The Bible is about a King, His Kingdom and His royal family. His royal family is a Kingdom of sons, both male and female.

There is neither Jew nor Greek, there is neither bond nor free, there is neither male nor female: for ye are all one in Christ Jesus.- Galatians 3:28

King Jesus did not come to planet earth to bring a religious system, but He came to bring a Kingdom. The Bible is about a King, who came here to bring a Kingdom and reproduce a family of sons.

> *And he hath on his vesture and on his thigh a name written, King Of Kings, And Lord Of Lords.- Revelation 19:16*

Jesus' Kingdom is the only one in the world where all of its citizens are royal kings.

> *Being born again, not of corruptible seed, but of incorruptible, by the word of God, which liveth and abideth for ever.- 1 Peter 1:23*

The incorruptible seed that was planted inside of you at new birth can reproduce after its kind. This incorruptible, royal seed of King Jesus will produce a king in you that looks just like Him.

> *For it became him, for whom are all things, and by whom are all things, in bringing many sons unto glory, to make the captain of their salvation perfect through sufferings. - Hebrews 2:10*

So impressed with the first King that He sent into the earth, our Heavenly Father brought many sons into that same glory as Jesus. Salvation was never meant to be a ticket to get into Heaven, or an opportunity to just get your life right. Salvation is about restoring God's original purpose and intent for your life so you can be restored into the Kingdom as kings and priests.

And the earth brought forth grass, and herb yielding seed after his kind, and the tree yielding fruit, whose seed was in itself, after his kind: and God saw that it was good. - Genesis 1:12

And let us not be weary in well doing: for in due season we shall reap, if we faint not. - Galatians 6:9

Let's look at the law of sowing and reaping. We know that whatsoever a man sows, that he will also reap. The Father sowed Jesus into the earth and He waits for a harvest of sons, who are kings, that will be just like Jesus. These kings will heal like Jesus, deliver like Jesus, raise the dead like Jesus, cast out devils like Jesus, and transform lives just like their older brother Jesus.

For both he that sanctifieth and they who are sanctified are all of one: for which cause he is not ashamed to call them brethren. - Hebrews 2:11

Currently, the Father is raising up a family of kings who Jesus is not ashamed to call His brothers.

But if the Spirit of him that raised up Jesus from the dead dwell in you, he that raised up Christ from the dead shall also quicken your mortal bodies by his Spirit that dwelleth in you. - Romans 8:11

The same Spirit that was in Jesus is the same Spirit in the body of Christ, not a different spirit, but the same, identical Spirit.

And hast made us unto our God kings and priests: and we shall reign on the earth. - Revelation 5:10

If we suffer, we shall also reign with him: if we deny him, he also will deny us. - 2 Timothy 2:12

As a young boy, I grew up in religion. Religion has hijacked the church of her true identity in Christ as kings.

RELIGION CANNOT GIVE MAN HIS TRUE IDENTITY AND PURPOSE IN CHRIST.

As kings, we are called to rule and reign with King Jesus in the earth in this life. Religion cannot give man his true identity and purpose in Christ. Therefore, mankind will always look for a means of escape out of his circumstances. As a result, religion created an any-minute rapture with the endeavor to avoid the troubles we face in this hostile world that we were born into. Jesus did not fill you with Heaven's Holy Ghost to leave the planet, but to transform it with the power of God. We are overcomers and not copper-outers.

The Spirit of the Lord is upon me, because he hath anointed me to preach the gospel to the poor; he hath sent me to heal the brokenhearted, to preach deliverance

> *to the captives, and recovering of sight to the blind, to set at liberty them that are bruised, to preach the acceptable year of the Lord. - Luke 4:18-19*

The Holy Ghost anointing upon a believer's life was not given to him to go to Heaven, but to transform the earth as we know it and bring the Kingdom of God into the planet. The anointing upon a believer never leaves the planet, but was given to him to transform the planet. Elijah went up, but his mantle stayed in the earth and came upon his spiritual son, Elisha. When King Jesus ascended into the Heavens in Acts chapter 1, Jesus went up, but His Holy Ghost mantle stayed in the earth and fell upon 120 in an upper room in Acts chapter 2.

> *And it shall come to pass in that day, that his burden shall be taken away from off thy shoulder, and his yoke from off thy neck, and the yoke shall be destroyed because of the anointing.- Isaiah 10:27*

The anointing was given to you and me to break yolks, not to find a way to go to Heaven. Heaven is doing okay; there is no sickness there, there is no lack there, there is no pain or suffering in Heaven. But just like it was with Jesus, the Spirit of the Lord is upon us because (a word of purpose) He has anointed us for the blind, the bound, the beggar, the broken, and the bruised. Simply stated, the anointing of the Holy Ghost is the Spirit of the Son worked into your life. Gifts are given to us by the Holy Spirit, but the anointing is more than a gift. It's the presence of the Lord rubbed in and worked into your very person; it is the very DNA of Christ in your life. More than a gift from the Giver, it is the Giver of the gifts operating in your life.

> *But the anointing which ye have received of him abideth in you, and ye need not that any man teach you: but as the same anointing teacheth you of all things, and is truth, and is no lie, and even as it hath taught you, ye shall abide in him. - 1 John 2:27*

The nine gifts of the Spirit work in us and through us as the Spirit wills, but the anointing of God abides in us and doesn't leave. The anointing quickens every aspect of your life; He anoints your thoughts, mind, vision, intellect, work, and speech. Everything becomes heightened in the anointing because it's supernatural in its properties.

> *Pilate therefore said unto him, Art thou a king then? Jesus answered, Thou sayest that I am a king. To this end was I born, and for this cause came I into the world, that I should bear witness unto the truth. Every one that is of the truth heareth my voice. - John 18:37*

Jesus was asked by Pilate, the Roman governor, "Are you a king?" And Jesus responded, "I am a King, and this was why I was born and for this cause have I come into the world." I was always taught as a young boy that Jesus came as our Savior and while that is true, there's so much more why Jesus came into the earth. He came foremost as a King. In this position, He saved, healed, delivered, and redeemed mankind. Jesus knew who He was and His assignment in the earth.

We live in a world filled with people who are living out of a mistaken identity. They don't know who they are and why they're in the planet. It's sad to say, even most Christians do not know who they are, what they have, and what they're assigned to do. This book introduces the reader to their true identity in Christ Jesus as kings and priests. We were born into a world that requires different identifications for multiple purposes and benefits. For example, if you wish to drive a car in the United States, you are required to have a driver's license. Without it, you may not drive a car, therefore missing out on the wonderful benefit of driving. Likewise, it is the same in the Spirit. You can be saved, but if you lack the right form of identification, you will miss the benefits and privileges that God has purposed for you to walk in. Imagine trying to access the Canadian border from the United States without the proper identification; you would be denied access to Canada. Your driver's license or your birth certificate are not sufficient because you're required to have a passport. When you receive Christ into your life and become a new creation, this is your spiritual birth certificate. But it is not enough to access all the riches in glories in Christ's Kingdom. You will need your identification as a king to access the realm of dominion.

Religion has robbed man of his true identity in Christ through identity theft. In the past, the charismatic, Pentecostal season granted us the privilege of functioning as priests unto our God. Your identification as a priest empowers you to worship, pray, and have an intimate relationship with the Lord Jesus Christ. Our priestly anointing also empowers us to minister to mankind, revealing God's love, mercy, and grace to all who are in need. As priests, we create vision, but as kings, we create provision. Kings have the power to create wealth and to attract wealth. When King Jesus was born, kings came from the Far East and laid their wealth at His feet. As kings are born in this season, wealth will be attracted to them so they can advance the Kingdom of God and fulfill their assignments.

Acts chapter 19 reveals a wonderful story, revealing this principle of proper identification. The Lord was performing special miracles at the hands of the Apostle Paul. So powerful were these miracles that they took pieces of cloth from Paul and sent them to those who were diseased and tormented by evil spirits and all were delivered. There were seven sons of Sceva, (a chief of the priests in the Levitical order) who watched Paul perform these miracles. They thought they would imitate what Paul did by attempting to cast out an evil spirit from a man. The seven men were a part of the Levitical priesthood, which came out of the Old Testament order. Paul was part of a New Testament priesthood, after the order of Melchizedek, an order of kings and priests. Not only did Paul have compassion for mankind as a priest, but he had the authority of a king to deliver them. The sons of Sceva were priests only, without the authority to deliver the possessed man of his demons. They did not have the right identification in the Spirit. Without the proper identification, they could not outrank the demons of that day. Your authority resides in your identification. We must examine who we are in Christ. Do not permit people who don't know who they are to determine who you are.

THE KINGLY ANOINTING GIVES YOU POWER TO RULE AND REIGN OVER YOUR SPHERE OF INFLUENCE.

The kingly anointing gives you power to rule and reign over your sphere of influence. To reign simply means to change things. And the highest form of rule is self-rule. If we cannot take dominion over our own lives within, how can we take dominion without? It's important that through the Spirit of the Living God that we take dominion over our bodies, our thoughts, our finances, our children, our diets, our attitudes, and even our mouths. All dominion flows out of your identity and your state of being.

Keep thy heart with all diligence; for out of it are the issues of life. - Proverbs 4:23

Out of a Kingdom consciousness, your heart will flow out the issues of life. In the Kingdom of God, we don't look for a blessing; the blessing flows out of the heart. Your world is an outflow of your heart. The Lord said through the prophet Malachi that He will open YOU, the windows of Heaven, and pour YOU out a blessing! I grew up in church hearing that God would open up some window in Heaven and pour out a blessing on us. But that's not what this passage says. It says He will open YOU as the window of Heaven and pour YOU out as a blessing. The saints are the windows of Heaven and sinners are the gates of hell. Jesus said, "Out of the mist of your belly shall flow rivers of living waters." In this Kingdom season, the blessing is not just coming to you, but through you. Power is given to a saint to be given away; we are given power to empower others. Stay full of the Spirit of God and He will continually pour you out into the lives of others. You'll never know what you have until you find a place to pour it out.

Our kingly anointing gives us dominion over our enemies, empowers us to create wealth, and empowers us to possess land and take territory. The Old Testament priests could not inherit land, but kings could possess land as part of their conquest. The earth is the Lord's and the fullness thereof. Jesus said, "Blessed are the meek for they shall inherit the earth." The word meek does not mean weak, but to be humble. Jesus was meek and lowly of heart. The word meek in Hebrew means: to be chastened, dealt harshly with, and seized by force; it means to be afflicted, be bound, to stoop or be low. Moses was the meekest man in the earth.

> *Now the man Moses was very meek, above all the men which were upon the face of the earth. - Numbers 12:3*

The Lord stripped Moses of all his ego during his wilderness experience. God is going to use empty, worn-out, broken people in the coming moves of the Spirit. To recover the earth, it will require the spirit of humility and not pride. Who do you think the Lord would have as custodians of His property, the saints, or the sinners?

> *Ask of me, and I shall give thee the heathen for thine inheritance, and the uttermost parts of the earth for thy possession. - Psalms 2:8*

Every major war that has been fought has been over land. So God is raising up kings to possess the land; there has always been a battle over land. Never give up your pursuit of land acquisition. Get a vision for acquiring it. If it's a drug house, buy it and convert it for Kingdom use because the Kingdom has need of it. If it's a bar, buy it and renovate it for Kingdom purposes. Don't let its current use keep you away from you possessing it. God will redeem the land, sanctify it, and it will radiate the character of His Kingdom. Both flower shops that my wife and I own stand on properties that my ancestors once possessed over 100 years ago. The Lord has redeemed the land and now it is being used to reflect the glory of God in and through our businesses.

They shall not labour in vain, nor bring forth for trouble; for they are the seed of the blessed of the Lord, and their offspring with them. - Isaiah 65:23

The Prophet Isaiah said kings will come out of the Messianic Seed, and that is Christ in you! Therefore, your children and children's children will be kings. This royal seed produces kings. As priests and kings, we determine the atmosphere that we will live in everyday. We take dominion by taking atmospheres. The atmosphere should be filled with righteousness, peace, and joy. We determine the measure of glory that other people will experience. People must submit to the level of glory that you bring into a room. People will submit to the greater glory in a room. As priests and kings, we govern the atmospheres that other people enter. For instance, David possessed a greater glory than Saul and the demons in Saul had to submit to the presence that David carried. Similarly, people will submit to the presence that you carry as a king in God's Kingdom. Dominion is not ruling over people, but ruling over atmospheres, environments, principalities, and powers that be. Kings control three things: environments, emotions, and energy. What do you leave in a room when you exit? Is it passion, vision, hope, faith, encouragement, fire, and glory? Do you lead people into a greater glory? Do you lead them into divine encounters? Moses had a divine encounter with a burning bush on Mount Sinai. God then sent him to deliver 3 million people out of Egypt. Moses was excited for them to experience the God that he had experienced at Mount Sinai, so that was their first stop after leaving Egypt. What's amazing is that he did not bring them to the same encounter that he had. Moses encountered a burning bush, but when he brought the 3 million Israelites to Mount Sinai, the entire mountain was on fire! We should bring people to a greater glory than what we've experienced. We should lead the next generation to God and to something much bigger than we've ever known. They should know the exceeding greatness of His power. As kings, you never need to google directions into the glory of God because as kings we live there. Hell cannot function in the wrong atmospheres; as kings, we are assigned to take dominion over territory and over atmospheres.

> *And Jesus, immediately knowing in himself that virtue had gone out of him, turned him about in the press, and said, Who touched my clothes? - Mark 5:30*
>
> *And the whole multitude sought to touch him: for there went virtue out of him, and healed them all. - Luke 6:19*

What do people get when they touch your life? Do they get bitterness, criticism, anger, selfishness, strife, and retaliation? Or do they receive virtue, righteousness, love, joy, peace, healing, gentleness, and goodness? May the virtue of Christ flow through you as a king in His Kingdom, touching lives and changing atmospheres.

And God said, Let us make man in our image, after our likeness: and let them have dominion over the fish of the sea, and over the fowl of the air, and over the cattle, and over all the earth, and over every creeping thing that creepeth upon the earth. - Genesis 1:26

Dominion flows out of our identity in Christ. When your true image is restored, dominion is restored.

CHAPTER 3

The Priesthood Is Changing

And the child Samuel ministered unto the Lord before Eli. And the word of the Lord was precious in those days; there was no open vision. And it came to pass at that time, when Eli was laid down in his place, and his eyes began to wax dim, that he could not see; And ere the lamp of God went out in the temple of the Lord, where the ark of God was, and Samuel was laid down to sleep; That the Lord called Samuel: and he answered, Here am I. - 1 Samuel 3:1-4

And I will raise me up a faithful priest, that shall do according to that which is in mine heart and in my mind: and I will build him a sure house; and he shall walk before mine anointed for ever. - 1 Samuel 2:35

In the days of Eli, high priest of Israel, the Word of the

Lord was precious, or very rare. In those days, with no open revelation, Eli seemed to be content with his life. The Bible says his eyes waxed dim and he could no longer see. Eli lost his vision like many pastors have in this present day. The time had come for the Lord to change the priesthood from a corrupt, polluted ministry to a faithful priesthood carrying the heart and mind of God. Samuel embodied this new, emerging priesthood that the Lord was raising up. Samuel would also be a kingmaker to elevate and anoint David as a king and priest, thus establishing God's new order in the earth. Part of David's assignment would be to recover the Ark of God to its rightful place in Zion.

In the days of Eli's priesthood, the Ark had departed from Israel. In rich allegory, the Ark of God symbolized the glory and presence of God and revealed His covenant-keeping nature. Finally, it represents God's government in the earth. On one occasion, Israel went to battle against the Philistines. Per usual, the elders called for the Ark of the Covenant, trusting that God would fight their battles for them as He had in past battles. The high priest Eli and his sons, Hophni and Phineas, however, treated the Ark superstitiously, like a lucky charm or a rabbit's foot. Refusing to repent, they thought they could still use the methods of God to win their battles while maintaining their sinful condition.

The Bible describes Eli's sons as men who didn't know God. They never fostered a personal relationship with Him. Daniel described those who know their God shall be strong and do great exploits. Knowing Him comes first; strength and doing exploits follows. Real power is measured by how much we love the Lord. Eli's sons did not have a presence driven life nor did they love God; therefore, they did not possess the power needed to win the battle. It's amazing how people want all the benefits of the Kingdom of God without a covenant relationship with Him. The most militant thing you can do is have an intimate relationship with King Jesus! Without an intimate relationship with the Lord and holiness, no one can presumptuously utilize the things of God. You cannot live before a holy God while living an unholy life. You will have two choices: get holy to live with God or get rid of God. What does holiness mean? It means that I am 100% His, a relationship that we must cultivate every single day of our lives.

God left His people because they took Him for granted and became familiar with Him, which cost them a reverential fear for the things of God. We want God to move, but when He does, it really can be a very terrifying experience. God demands change equating to repentance, which means "to fit into place." Please understand this, God is not American; He is sovereign. Seeker-friendly churches of our day have become Americanized by being more interested in pleasing man than pleasing the Lord. These churches have tried to make God in their image instead of them being transformed into His image. Two churches exist in the world today: prophetic churches and performance churches. The first entertains God, and the second entertains men. God is not American in that He doesn't ask for opinions or our vote. The Kingdom of God does not offer multiple choice answers to questions. Two options exist: obey or disobey. Either we're in or we're out, willing or not willing; we can choose good or evil, life or death and blessing or cursing. Choose well.

TWO CHURCHES EXIST IN THE WORLD TODAY: PROPHETIC CHURCHES AND PERFORMANCE CHURCHES.

The church at large has tried to make God in their image; we want Him to think, act, and live like us. A hyper grace message has infiltrated the American church with the spirit of Hophni and Phineas. Every time today's church gets in trouble, they believe they can just call on God and He will magically solve all their problems. This spirit has driven God out of churches instead of inviting Him into our churches. Grace is not freedom to do whatever we want, but a life force that empowers us to do the God thing.

Not purloining, but shewing all good fidelity; that

they may adorn the doctrine of God our Saviour in all things. For the grace of God that bringeth salvation hath appeared to all men, teaching us that, denying ungodliness and worldly lusts, we should live soberly, righteously, and godly, in this present world; Looking for that blessed hope, and the glorious appearing of the great God and our Saviour, Jesus Christ. - Titus 2:10-13

Grace teaches us to live righteous lives. Grace is a revelation that you and I cannot do anything on our own. Grace has a nickname known as "God's ability."

Follow peace with all men, and holiness, without which no man shall see the Lord. - Hebrews 12:14

Holiness prepares God's people for a visitation from the Lord, inviting the glory of God into your life. The grace of God upon you welcomes salvation, healing, and deliverance into your home. It invites all the blessings and benefits of the Kingdom into your house. We will see this in the life of Obededom in the next chapter. Grace signals Heaven saying, "We are ready for you, Lord; we are ready for more of You!"

The children of Israel lost the presence of God because they were not willing to change. In God's economy, we are presently changing seasons which demands a change of hearts. God cannot live with His people, but presently He is seeking out a people who He can live with and who will become His habitation. This is not a day that God just wants to visit His people, but He wants us to be His habitation. With the days of visitation behind us, the days of habitation are right before us. God will find people willing to be His holy habitation. Let me explain the difference between visitation and habitation. If I called you on the phone to tell you I was coming to visit your family for three days, it wouldn't take a lot of preparation for my three-day visit. You could shove some things under the bed and hide other things in the closet for my short stay. But if I told you I was coming to move in permanently, the preparation would be more intense. You may need to add on a room or transform one that would accommodate me to move in permanently. In previous moves of God, there were visitations that required little preparation. But our preparation today requires intensity because God is not just coming to visit us; He is preparing a people who will be His habitation.

And are built upon the foundation of the apostles and prophets, Jesus Christ himself being the chief corner stone; In whom all the building fitly framed together groweth unto a holy temple in the Lord: In whom ye also are builded together for a habitation of God through the Spirit. - Ephesians 2:20-22

Repenting means we must match, fit in, and go into the right position. People in the world have come to our churches expecting to see God since His name is written on our churches: Assembly of God, Church of God, The

House of God, just to name a few. If you come to my home, you expect to meet Mark Kauffman because it's my house. Because I live there, you would expect to see and meet me. Although His name is on the house, and people come expecting to find Him, instead they meet actors, singers, entertainers, and great speakers. In the end, these seekers ask, "Where is God?"

While the Ark was stolen and missing for over 20 years, the Israelites learned to live without God. The church of America makes excuses for not having God in our midst. They preach a message that contradicts Scripture. They say God is in Heaven and you'll meet Him there someday, when you pass from this life to the next. We talk about Him like He's on vacation somewhere when He is right here with us. The change of the priesthood in this new season involves God cleansing a polluted priesthood and raising up a new one. I want to keep His presence at any cost; I want the Ark of His presence back in church! Let's rise like King David, go fetch the Ark and bring it to its rightful place among the people of God. It will take an emerging king and priest's ministry to bring the presence of God back to its rightful place.

Repentance is not just an apology for messing up. Rather, it's a deep conviction of our heart that produces a new way of thinking and acting. We cannot go on the battlefield without the presence of God. Quoting scriptures and using Jesus' Name will not defeat our enemies if there's not a presence behind those decrees. Many battles we have lost have been orchestrated by God to teach us lessons. He is saying, "Without My presence you will never win the battle, you will never be an overcomer; you will never be victorious without me." Without His presence, we are no match for our enemies. It's His presence that empowers us to outrank them. Intimacy with Jesus anoints us to be victorious. We cannot live without a covenant relationship with King Jesus. When Hophni and Phineas called for the Ark, the Philistines cried out in fear in remembrance of what the Ark had done in the past. The Ark parted the Jordan and brought down Jericho's walls! When Israel's God showed up, everything changed. When God shows up, He doesn't care about your pedigree, age, color, bank account, who your grandma and grandpa were, what church you belong to, how long you've been saved, or what the church board says.

But this time, for the Israelites, God did not show up and show off on their behalf because of their presumptuous spirits. The Philistines took the Ark and carried it away to their homeland. What were the Israelites going to do without their God now? What do you do when you live one way in church and another way at home? When we are not willing to live a Kingdom life, a surrendered and obedient life to God, we forfeit the benefits and blessings of Christ's Kingdom.

> *And when the ark of the covenant of the Lord came into the camp, all Israel shouted with a great shout, so that the earth rang again. And when the Philistines heard the noise of the shout, they said, What meaneth the noise of this great shout in the camp of the Hebrews? And they understood that the ark of the Lord was come into the camp. And the Philistines were afraid, for they said, God is coming into the camp. And they said, Woe unto us! For there hath not been such a thing heretofore.*
> *- 1 Samuel 4:5-7*

The children of Israel shouted when the Ark appeared on the battlefield, but God was not in their shout. Likewise, we can come to church, praise the Lord, shout and holler all we want on Sunday, but if there is not a presence backing that shout, God will not be in it.

> *And the Philistines took the ark of God and brought it from Ebenezer unto Ashdod. When the Philistines took the ark of God, they brought it into the house of Dagon, and set it by Dagon. And when they of Ashdod arose early on the morrow, behold, Dagon was fallen upon his face to the earth before the ark of the Lord. And they took Dagon, and set him in his place again. And when they arose early on the morrow morning, behold, Dagon was fallen upon his face to the ground before the ark of the Lord; and the head of Dagon and both the palms of his hands were cut off upon the threshold; only the stump of Dagon was left to him. Therefore, neither the priests of Dagon, nor any that come into Dagon's house, tread on the threshold of Dagon in Ashdod unto this day. - 1 Samuel 5:1-5*

The Philistines put the Ark in the temple of Dagon. Dagon was a Philistine god that was half man and half fish. You can't put God's presence where something fishy is going on. His presence will not settle around fishy things where man's carnality rules. We cannot believe for one minute that we are saved, filled with Heaven's Holy Ghost and have made Jesus the Lord over our lives, and simultaneously think that He won't deal with the fishy things in our lives. It's like getting married and thinking you can have another relationship with someone other than your spouse.

The first manifestation of God's presence was not miraculous but showed up in a shaking! No one is ever fully ready for this—when God first comes to shake what needs to be shaken. God will always shake what is out of order. If there is a shaking going on, it's not from an angry God, but from a loving, merciful God who will not share us with anything that is not compatible with Him. God comes after the fishy things that don't smell right. When God is shaking your life, be sure to not dust off and pick up what God is tearing down. He wants His temple to be filled with Him and Him alone. He doesn't care if you approve or not. He comes to knock down what is not supposed to be in His temple. But if you try to raise it back up, He will come again and again. He loves you enough to keep coming after you.

Just like God took out Dagon, God will take everything

out of your life that opposes His Word. This is a season where God is taking dominion over everything that opposes His will and Word in your life. Disease, sickness, lack, fear, lethargy, lukewarmness and everything that opposes you must leave. He is coming to take these things out of His temple, for they keep Him from being Lord of your life. Either He's Lord of all or He is not Lord at all.

The next morning, after the Ark of God was placed beside Dagon, the god's head and hands were broken off. God is coming to cut off the arms of the enemy so that he can no longer work in your life. That day, Dagon had a terrible day. Presently, the Lord is cleansing and preparing our temples, and we are about to give hell a terrible day. Everything contrary to God must go in our lives. In this season, God is coming after every evil thing that's opposing you. Ready or not, here He comes! When the ark shows up, things will just fall off. In this season, God will knock down everything that keeps Him from being Lord in your life. The presence of God is going to get into our marriages, families, pocketbooks, churches, businesses, relationships, and our attitudes. He will shake everything that can be shaken. He is coming to cut the head off everything that controls us from being His Kingdom people. He is knocking down pride, jealousy, rebellion, bad attitudes, and negative speech. Don't try to put stuff together that God is tearing down.

God knows how to put you and me on our faces. Dagon fell forward, not backward. God will put us in the posture of worship. He is getting ready to cut the hands off the Dagon in your life. To me, this represents the enemy being forced to take his hands off your marriage, money, children, and health. The enemy's plans are about to be dismantled, and everything bows when God shows up! When the presence of God shows up, cancer bows, diabetes bow, depression bows, mental disorders bow, yes, everything bows at His presence.

For it is written, As I live, saith the Lord, every knee shall bow to me, and every tongue shall confess to God. - Romans 14:11

That at the name of Jesus every knee should bow, of things in heaven, and things in earth, and things under the earth. - Philippians 2:10

In the next chapter, we will see how King David restored the presence of God back to its rightful place. But en route to Mount Zion, God turned aside to visit a man by the name of Obededom. It's time for us to prepare for the Ark to turn aside. Ready or not, here He comes!

Chapter 4

Transitional Glory

Again, David gathered together all the chosen men of Israel, thirty thousand. And David arose, and went with all the people that were with him from Baale of Judah, to bring up from thence the ark of God, whose name is called by the name of the Lord of hosts that dwelleth between the cherubims. And they set the ark of God upon a new cart, and brought it out of the house of Abinadab that was in Gibeah: and Uzzah and Ahio, the sons of Abinadab, drove the new cart. And they brought it out of the house of Abinadab which was at Gibeah, accompanying the ark of God: and Ahio went before the ark. And David and all the house of Israel played before the Lord on all manner of instruments made of fir wood, even on harps, and on psalteries, and on timbrels, and on cornets, and on cymbals. And when they came to Nachon's threshingfloor, Uzzah put forth his hand to the ark of God, and took hold of it; for the oxen shook it. And the anger of the Lord was kindled against Uzzah; and God smote him there for his error; and there he died by the ark of God. And David was displeased, because the Lord had made a breach upon Uzzah: and he called the name of the place Perezuzzah to this day. And David was afraid of the Lord that day, and said, How shall the ark of the Lord come to me? So David would not remove the ark of the Lord unto him into the city of David: but David carried it aside into the house of Obededom the Gittite. And the ark of the Lord continued in the house of Obededom the Gittite three months: and the Lord blessed Obededom, and all his household. And it was told king David, saying, The Lord hath blessed the house of Obededom, and all that pertaineth unto him, because of the ark of God. So David went and brought up the ark of God from the house of Obededom into the city of David with gladness. - 2 Samuel 6:1-12

In the days of King Saul the Ark of God's presence was missing for over 20 years. David's first mission as king was to recover the Ark and return it to its rightful place at Mount Zion. Let me share this wonderful story with you about transitional glory. We are in a season in which I call IN BETWEEN. We are in between the Church age and the Kingdom age, between man's day and God's day, between the charismatic, Pentecostal season and the season of God's glorious Kingdom.

David's first attempt to bring the Ark back to its home base was done by setting it on an oxcart. An oxcart represents man-made systems and organizations that are not built to carry the presence of God. Oxcarts are made of boards and big wheels. The Ark was meant to be carried on the shoulders of a priesthood, representing plurality of ministry. Instead, they used an ox to drive the Ark back home, symbolizing a beastly system. In between the land of the Philistines and Mount Zion, the oxcart hit a speed bump in the road that shook the cart. Uzzah, son of Abinadab, reached out to steady the Ark and died. This speaks to me that we can't touch the things of God any way we want to. The church must recover our reverential fear for the things of God. David turns aside at Obededom's house, allowing him to park the Ark here until he found the due order to bring it back home. God would now dwell in a place called IN BETWEEN for three months. God always dwells in a place called IN BETWEEN. God told Israel I'll meet you in between the cherubs.

> *And I sought for a man among them, that should make up the hedge, and stand in the gap before me for the land, that I should not destroy it: but I found none. - Ezekiel 22:30*

Obededom was called to stand in the gap in the time of transition. God is always looking for someone to stand in the gap during transitional times. Obededom's house would entertain the presence of God in that day. It is my purpose in this chapter to locate the true church of Jesus Christ in this present hour. Before all of Israel viewed and experienced the presence of God, the Ark was carried aside into Obededom's house so God could bless him. We know that the whole earth will be filled with the glory of the Lord, but before the world experiences and sees the manifest presence of God, He must first turn aside to bless houses after the order of Obededom.

Let's look and see why God blessed this man. His name means worshiping servant. This worshiping servant would entertain the presence of God while David sought God's qualifications for how to transport the Ark. Worship is more than what we do on a Sunday morning in a church service; worship is a surrendered life. When Jesus met the woman at the well, He did not say that the Father was looking for people who worship; He said that the Father was looking for worshipers. There is quite a difference between the two. Every Sunday morning, churches are filled with worship; the question is: are there worshipers? Being a worshiper means we live a surrendered life every day for King Jesus. We worship God by how we treat our spouses, how we

GOD IS ALWAYS LOOKING FOR SOMEONE TO STAND IN THE GAP DURING TRANSITIONAL TIMES.

raise our children, our business ethics Monday through Friday, and how we live our life before King Jesus when no one is looking. That's real worship. Worship is a lifestyle whereby our speech, attitude, behavior, and conduct glorify God in everything we do. We worship by how we give, by how we serve, by our work, how we discipline our children, by how we honor our employees and employers. The old English word for worship is worth-ship, defined as "something of value, transported to, a giver to God." Our singing, clapping of hands, shouting, dancing, and playing instruments are only expressions of our worship. The truth of the matter is our lifestyle empowers our song. Worship is to be demonstrated out of our love for God 24 hours a day, 365 days a year. We worship Him in everything we do. True worship is when our lips and our life agree with Heaven; it's when our word and our walk are one. Your song has no power if there is no lifestyle backing it up. Displaying and demonstrating our love for our Heavenly Father is true worship. When men and women reconcile Sunday morning with Monday through Saturday, then they are a true worshiper. Whole life worship is living our lives out of our worship to God. A life of worship will make you compatible with the Lord.

Obededom was also a Gittite, which means the winepress. He lived in the place of pressure. Look at it this way in your life, many of you have lived in the winepress, presently existing under great pressure. Don't move from the place of pressure, for the Lord is coming to bless you at the winepress. In a city called Gath, his house was in the very hometown of Goliath's family. This represents the place of giant opposition, warfare, and affliction. Not only did Obededom live in the winepress, but he settled in the land of giant hostility. At the time that I wrote this book, there are so many in the body of Christ who have been in the place of pressure and surrounded by giant opposition, but be encouraged, for the Lord is coming to bless and favor you. Suddenly, unexpectedly, and unannounced, the Ark showed up! God visited a man who was a worshiping servant living in a place of great pressure. Because this worshiping servant pressed through tribulation, he become a candidate for a season of favor and blessing. The Bible says that God blessed all that pertained to this man. I believe that He got into everything in this house, including his marriage, family, health, and pocketbook. For all those faithful, worshiping servants in the season called IN BETWEEN, God is about to get into all your affairs. I don't know about you, but I want God to get in all my stuff; I want Him to invade my home and bless everything I have. In Hebrew, the word bless means to be endued with power for success, prosperity, longevity, provision, protection, glory, honor, and favor. Sign me up for that! If this chapter is ministering to you, hear this: do not move from the place of pressure, do not throw in the towel; He is coming to you now to bless and favor you so you can succeed.

God will bless you in the face of your enemies. God blessed this man, Obededom, and all that he had right in the face of giant opposition. The Psalmist said, "He will prepare a table for you right in the midst of your enemies." Those who sang your doxology and counted you out, those who mocked you and laughed at you, cursed and criticized you, will watch God bless you. The same ones that saw you go down in despair will be those who see you rise in success. God does not judge your enemies by putting cancer on them. No, the way He judges our enemies is by giving us massive success. God is about to show up in the most unlikely places, much like Gath. Suddenly, quickly, the blessing of the Lord will come to you.

How did the Lord bless Obededom and his family? God rewarded this worshiper by raising up his sons and grandsons to be mighty men of valor. They were able men for strength and service. Obededom was promoted by David as a doorkeeper of the Ark in Zion. He was promoted as a leader of leaders, with 68 leaders under his care. He is last mentioned in Scripture as a keeper of the temple. King David entrusted him to guard the gold that equated to over 2 billion dollars. All his eight sons were gatekeepers to the glory of the Lord. Obededom and his sons were best suited to open the temple gates. Worshiping servants in this present hour will qualify to open the Kingdom of Heaven and usher others into His presence. This place that we call IN BETWEEN is a place of testing and qualification for a new breed of worshiping servants who will qualify to entertain the presence of God. Be encouraged. He is about to bless His worshiping servants.

The ark of God represents God's manifest presence, but also His government. The government was placed upon His shoulders. Obededom opened his house up to God's government and it impacted generations. The presence of God must be recovered in these days, but that is not enough. People encounter His presence and go right back to their old lifestyle. I've seen people get healed by the miraculous power of God, yet return to their sinful lives. But when they encounter His Kingdom government, they will forever be transformed and changed. At this present time, the Lord is also restoring His government back to the body of Christ in order for lives to be eternally transformed. Your season of breaking will lead you into a season of blessing, and beyond the blessing is a season of building. The blessing of the Lord comes upon your life so you can build His Kingdom in the earth.

The Lord said unto my Lord, Sit thou at my right hand, until I make thine enemies thy footstool. - Psalms 110:1

This Scripture is like no other verse in the Bible. It is mentioned 8 times, which is the number for new beginnings.

Exalt ye the Lord our God and worship at his footstool; for he is holy. - Psalms 99:5

This Scripture reveals that the same place where our enemies become our footstool is where we worship! Wow, I find that very interesting. As worshiping servants, our enemies become our footstool to reach new realms in God. Your opposition is not a stumbling block, but a steppingstone to reach what you could not reach without them. When my son Christian Mark was a small boy, he couldn't reach the snacks that his mother had put up in the kitchen cabinet. He would get the footstool and climb up on the counter so he could reach what he could not reach alone. Moses would've never reached his destiny if it wasn't for a footstool by the name of Pharaoh. Joseph would've never reached His God-ordained purpose as prime minister without a footstool called his brothers. Gideon would've never fulfilled his calling without a footstool called the Midianites. The three Hebrew boys would've never fulfilled their assignment if it wasn't for a footstool called a fiery furnace. David would've never become king if it wasn't for the footstools called Goliath and Saul. Esther would've never fulfilled her purpose in God if it wasn't for a footstool called Haman. Daniel would've never been raised up to be governor if it wasn't for a footstool called the lion's den. There are things laid up for us in heavenly places that we will never receive without footstools.

A good man leaveth an inheritance to his children's children: and the wealth of the sinner is laid up for the just. - Proverbs 13:22

The Lord has allowed the wicked to store up wealth until the saints of God mature, overcome their enemies, and make their enemies their footstools so they can reach the wealth that is laid up to advance the Kingdom of God in their lives.

For a great door and effectual is opened unto me, and there are many adversaries. - 1 Corinthians 16:9

There was a great and effectual door opened for Paul, but he said there was also great adversity. Adversity is the hinges on which the door of opportunity swings wide. The king that is within you will not rest until all your enemies have become your footstool. It's time to bring the presence of God and His glory back to our homes, churches, businesses, cities, and nations. The whole earth is to be filled with the glory of the Lord. God and His predetermined purpose is relentless in His pursuit to favor and bless His worshiping servants.

Chapter 5

The Caleb Generation

Every new move of the Spirit of God requires a new type of grace leadership to spearhead the movement. It takes a certain breed of what I call "echelon leadership" to breakthrough into a new season. They possess a specific grace to overcome their enemies and transform the culture of their day. I believe that Moses, Joshua, and Caleb represent the grace leadership that has been evident in the church over the last 60 years.

The Moses generation administrated God's movements during the 1950s, the 1960s, and the 1970s. Then in the 1980s, the Joshua generation emerged and picked up the mantle to bring the church into a new season. Presently, we are coming into the season, which requires a leadership that operates in the spirit of the Kingdom of God. To be successful in this new Kingdom era, it will require the grace leadership that Caleb exemplified.

My father, Kenneth Kauffman, was part of the Moses generation. He carried the grace of Moses. His strong pastoral gift and courageous mantle led his congregation out of religion and into the new thing that God was doing in his day. I rededicated my life to the Lord in 1988, which was very close to the time that God began to raise up a new breed of leadership that many called the Joshua generation. This group prepared us to be a military might in God's Kingdom. I'm thankful for those who led as Moses and Joshua in our day, but as we now transition into this new Kingdom season, it will require the grace leadership of a company of Calebs.

Moses came out of the tribe of Levi; the Levites served the Lord as His priesthood. Joshua was an Ephraimite, and out of the Ephraimites came forth God's prophets. But Caleb came out of the tribe of Judah, and out of this tribe came forth THE KINGS. Once again, we can see the pattern regarding the restoration of the priestly, prophetic and kingly mantles back into the earth over the past 60 to 70 years. Let's examine how the Moses generation restored the priesthood to us. My father, a forerunner of that Moses generation, taught our church congregation how to function as priests, emphasizing worship, praise, prayer, servanthood, and developing an intimate relationship with the Lord Jesus Christ. Then came the Joshua generation in the 80s that restored the prophetic to the church. I remember in the early 1990s having open microphone prophetic meetings where we learned to grow and move in the prophetic.

Follow after charity, and desire spiritual gifts, but rather that ye may prophesy. - 1 Corinthians 14:1

And Moses said unto him, Enviest thou for my sake? Would God that all the Lord's people were prophets, and that the Lord would put his spirit upon them! - Numbers 11:29

The Joshuas in the last season taught us how to be a prophetic people who not only prophesied the Word of the Lord over individuals, but learned to flow in prophetic dreams and visions, move in prophetic worship and praise and live our lives prophetically before the Lord. We should be so thankful for our roots—growing up in the previous moves of the Spirit, grateful for all that God has developed within us over the years as we matured into our priestly and prophetic mantles. But now a new day has dawned where we bring our priestly and prophetic mantles with us and move in and grow comfortably into our fresh mantle as kings.

This is the Caleb generation, whereby we all can rule and reign as kings, priests, and prophets in the earth.

And hath made us kings and priests unto God and his Father; to him be glory and dominion for ever and ever. Amen. - Revelation 1:6

Until this present time, our churches have been filled with priests and prophets. We have been worshiping, praising, and praying as priests, as well as prophesying over each other as a prophetic people. But we've not been ruling and reigning as kings over our circumstances and in our world. The answer to our personal problems and the present issues in our world cannot be resolved without this kingly mantle of dominion. Our kingly mantle empowers us to rule over sickness, disease, poverty, mammon, and every other enemy that opposes Christ's Kingdom. You cannot become a king in a church that only has priests and prophets; you must find a church that has kingmakers.

The church has attempted to commission men and women into the seven spheres of society (business, media, family, religion, government, education, and arts and entertainment). These seven spheres shape the culture of our world. Our assignment is to transform society with the culture of Heaven, which requires more than priestly and prophetic mantles; it demands the kingly mantle. I believe this is the reason we have seen very little success in transforming these seven mountains. We have prematurely commissioned men and women into their mountains without their kingly mantles. But these are exciting days in which God has raised up Samuels from the charismatic movement with a kingmaker anointing to equip, train, and prepare a generation of kings to rule on top of the seven mountains. We are in training for reigning! This Third and Final Reformation restores this missing key ingredient to the Kingdom of God known as the kingly mantle. Remember that our pattern is Jesus. As He is all three roles of king, priest, and prophet, so are we in this present world. It's my prayer that the words penned in this book will stir up the king that is resident in your spirit man. You will have to find a kingmaker who can help you push this king out of your spiritual womb.

So let's look at what this kingly mantle embodies so we can operate as kings in these seven societal spheres. Caleb, who came out of Judah, the tribe of kings, represents a new breed of leader that God is raising up today. Caleb not only took out giants, but he also took mountains. Caleb's kingly mantle outranked all his enemies. I truly believe that occurred in Joshua chapter 13, where the mantle was passed from Joshua to Caleb. The book of Joshua could be divided into two books: chapters 1 through 12 and chapters 13 through 24. In the first 12 chapters, the Israelites conquered the land and in the last 12 chapters; they divided the land. Unconquered territory remained when the mantle was passed to Caleb, but the time had come to divide the land as an inheritance to the children of Israel. Joshua was well stricken in years at this time. Now Caleb waited for his turn, and finally, after 45 years, he received his portion of the inheritance, which was the land of Hebron.

Joshua is a type of Jesus Christ who is the Testator of a New Testament and will. Jesus' death on Calvary's cross and resurrection from the dead made Him the administrator of His own will and testament.

> *Giving thanks unto the Father, which hath made us meet to be partakers of the inheritance of the saints in light. - Colossians 1:12*

> *And if children, then heirs; heirs of God, and joint-heirs with Christ; if so, be that we suffer with him, that we may be also glorified together. - Romans 8:17*

To receive a harvest in Christ's Kingdom, you must sow something. If you want a promise, you will have to overcome something. But if you want an inheritance, you only have to be someone, an heir.

> *In whom ye also trusted, after that ye heard the word of truth, the gospel of your salvation: in whom also after that ye believed, ye were sealed with that holy Spirit of promise, Which is the earnest of our inheritance until the redemption of the purchased possession, unto the praise of his glory. - Ephesians 1:13,14*

This powerful passage of Scripture describes the baptism of the Holy Ghost as a pledge and a promise; it is the earnest of our inheritance. In banking terms, earnest means a portion of something given or done in advance as a pledge of the remainder. In short, it a vow that there is more to come. For example, when buying a home, you put a down payment on the house, assuring the bank that there is more money on the way. The earnest is the down payment for the purchased possession. The baptism of the Holy Ghost is our earnest. He is a pledge, a promise, that there is so much more to come in Christ for you as a believer. If the down payment of the Holy Ghost is that good, what will the full inheritance look like? Your Pentecostal experience in Christ is a guarantee of a greater glory to come in Christ Jesus, our Lord. If you recall when the 12 spies crossed over into the Promised Land, they cut down branches and placed a cluster of grapes on them. This was evidence for the

THE CALEB GENERATION WILL LIVE A HOLY, SURRENDERED LIFE TO KING JESUS.

children of Israel of what was in store for them once they crossed over the Jordan and into that land. It was a foretaste of their inheritance. This is the type and shadow of the baptism of the Holy Spirit, a foretaste of greater things to come in Christ. Don't settle for less than God's best; there is so much more that Christ has for each one of us. You have more than you think you have, you can do more than you think you can ever do, and you will be more than you think you can ever be. It is the Caleb generation that will lead the church into its divine inheritance in Christ Jesus. Therefore, our prayer should be in this season, "Dear Lord, that which You have foreordained for me from the foundation of the world for this present hour, as my inheritance, I ask You to release it in Jesus' Name. As heirs of God and joint heirs with Jesus Christ, our Lord and Savior, dispense my inheritance now, according to Your desire and divine will that I may accomplish the purpose and plan that You have for me in this present world."

> *But my servant Caleb, because he had another spirit with him, and hath followed me fully, him will I bring into the land whereinto he went; and his seed shall possess it. - Numbers 14:24*

Caleb had another spirit or shall we say, another anointing.

> *And I will pray the Father, and he shall give you another Comforter, that he may abide with you forever. - John 14:16*

The Caleb generation has another anointing that is kingly and rests upon them. Now let's look at the mantle of Caleb.

> *Save Caleb the son of Jephunneh the Kenezite, and Joshua the son of Nun: for they have wholly followed the Lord. - Numbers 32:12*

To become a part of a Caleb generation, you cannot look

back, turn back, throw in the towel and quit. Instead, you must wholly follow Him all the way into your destiny. The Caleb generation will live a holy, surrendered life to King Jesus. Holiness, simply stated, means, I AM HIS.

> *And now, behold, the Lord hath kept me alive, as he said, these forty and five years, even since the Lord spake this word unto Moses, while the children of Israel wandered in the wilderness. - Joshua 14:10a*

The anointing on Caleb kept him alive through the wilderness journey and this anointing will bring that same life to you and all those around you. The Spirit of God that raised Christ from the dead that now dwells in you and me will quicken and make alive even our mortal bodies. This life is so powerful that it swallows up death, fear, worry, sickness, and every opposing force that will come against you.

> *As yet I am as strong this day as I was in the day that Moses sent me: as my strength was then, even so is my strength now, for war, both to go out, and to come in. - Joshua 14:11*

The Caleb anointing can even restore your youth back to you. Caleb, at the age of 85, was renewed in his body that he was as strong as he was at 40 years of age. This Caleb anointing will empower and strengthen you to fulfill and finish your destiny strong.

> *Now therefore give me this mountain, whereof the Lord spake in that day. - Joshua 14:12a*

This kingly anointing will also equip you and empower you to rule over the seven mountains/spheres of society that you were called to. Giving you the edge, it will tip the scales in your favor.

> *If so be the Lord will be with me, then I shall be able to drive them out, as the Lord said. - Joshua 14:12b*

It is this Caleb, kingly anointing, that will provide you with power from on high to drive out the giants in the land and overcome all your enemies.

Caleb's name means dog. A synonym for tenacious is the word dogged. The Caleb generation is very tenacious. They will not relent, and are very persistent; they want their mountain, and they want it now! Persistence brings success! I have never met a successful person who did not have a spirit of persistence. Persistence always comes with great reward. In Caleb's day, dogs were not domesticated; they were wild animals that ran the streets. This Caleb generation has not been domesticated by religion and refuses to follow the traditions of men, but they will wholly follow God and will not live passive, predictable lives. The Caleb generation is on a Kingdom conquest, refusing to take no for an answer and pursuing the promises of God until they see them fulfilled in their lives. As the old saying goes, "Every dog has its day." This is the day of the Caleb generation. The Kingdom is going to the dogs!

CHAPTER 6

The Kingdom of God

And when he was demanded of the Pharisees, when the kingdom of God should come, he answered them and said, The kingdom of God cometh not with observation: Neither shall they say, Lo here! Or, lo there! For, behold, the kingdom of God is within you. - Luke 17:20-21

For the kingdom of God is not meat and drink; but righteousness, and peace, and joy in the Holy Ghost. - Romans 14:17

Many believers have a difficult time seeing the Kingdom of God and feel challenged by a Kingdom culture because of their indoctrinated background in religion. To define it, the Kingdom of God is the governmental rule and reign of King Jesus in and through His church in the earth. It is the realm of the authority of the King, and it is the territory of citizens where the King rules. The Kingdom is where God's perfect will and His rule is done in the earth as it is in Heaven through the church of Jesus Christ. It is not a when, but a who! We are not meant to look for or wait for the Kingdom, but it is always personified into a people, finding its fulfillment in them. Jesus never taught a message called Christianity, but He taught the Kingdom. The Kingdom of God is not God's latest plan, but His eternal plan. Not intended for halfhearted people, this place is reserved for a people that are sold out to the King and His Kingdom.

In the Greek, Kingdom is the word "basileia" which means sovereignty, royal power, and dominion. Vine's dictionary defines the word as royalty and rule, stemming from a root word that is rendered as walk or foot. The Kingdom of God is a walk, a lifestyle that we live and demonstrate in our present world. It does not just come in word, but in power.

For the kingdom of God is not in word, but in power. - 1 Corinthians 4:20

Not to be confused as an event or a coming attraction in the future, the Kingdom is within you right NOW as righteousness, peace, and joy in the Holy Ghost. It's in the Holy Ghost and He dwells in you. It is not an external event, but an internal reality. God's Kingdom is a culture where righteousness (right relationship), peace (infectious domination), and joy (lifestyle expression) are manifested in and through your life. This Kingdom is meant to bleed out of you into your families, homes, schools, businesses, government, churches, neighborhoods and into cities. Not relating to what you have, what you can do, or what you can get, the Kingdom is about who you are. It is well defined as a lifestyle in Christ. Jesus said you will know His followers by their fruit. As a Kingdom of priests, we move in both the gifts and the fruit of the Spirit. The fruit is the character of the Kingdom involving love, joy, peace, long-suffering, gentleness, goodness, faith, meekness, and temperance. The gifts are the authority of the Kingdom, the word of wisdom, the word of knowledge, faith, gifts of healing, miracles, prophecy, discerning of spirits, tongues, and interpretation of tongues. The nine gifts and the nine fruits speak to us of a well-balanced ministry. The gifts of the Spirit can be divided into three categories that explain how the kings that are emerging in this day will speak, think, and act like God.

THE KINGDOM OF GOD IS THE GOVERNMENTAL RULE AND REIGN OF KING JESUS IN AND THROUGH HIS CHURCH IN THE EARTH.

THREE CATEGORIES OF THE GIFTS OF THE SPIRIT

- **We speak like God:** Speaking in tongues, the interpretation of tongues, and prophecy
- **We think like God:** The word of wisdom, the word of knowledge, and the discerning of spirits
- **We act like God:** The gifts of healing, gift of faith, and the working miracles

This Kingdom of God upon the earth is God's dream for families, churches, and every sphere of society. So many believers pray and dream of going to Heaven someday. Why? It's because their life on earth is not filled with the present reality of Heaven now. The only answer to the world's problems is the Kingdom of God! We don't have to die to go to Heaven, but we can experience days of Heaven upon the earth right now in the midst of a wicked and perverse generation. It will require the Kingdom of God to manifest in the earth through the church if we are to experience days of Heaven here. Kingdom people do not make Heaven their home, but they make their home like Heaven. Jesus shared about the Kingdom of Heaven and the Kingdom of God.

These two are not synonymous. The Kingdom of Heaven is what we belong to, while the Kingdom of God is the power and the authority that we walk in.

After this manner therefore pray ye: Our Father which art in heaven, Hallowed be thy name. Thy kingdom come, Thy will be done in earth, as it is in heaven. - Matthew 6:9,10

I find it very strange that the majority of the church is wanting to leave the planet to go to Heaven when Jesus taught us to pray the truth: Thy Kingdom COME, Thy will be done IN EARTH as it is in Heaven. While most Christians are wanting to evacuate the planet, He wants the Kingdom of Heaven upon the earth. It's never been Thy church go, but Thy Kingdom come! God is after the recovery of the earth, not the abandonment of it, regardless of what some theologians may say.

The Bible is about the King, His Kingdom, and His royal Kingdom family. This family is a Kingdom comprised of sons. The royal family of Jesus Christ is made up of kings and priests; Apostle Peter calls them a Royal Priesthood.

Ye also, as lively stones, are built up a spiritual house, an holy priesthood, to offer up spiritual sacrifices, acceptable to God by Jesus Christ.- 1 Peter 2:5

And from Jesus Christ, who is the faithful witness, and the first begotten of the dead, and the prince of the kings of the earth. Unto him that loved us, and washed us from our sins in his own blood, and hath made us kings and priests unto God and his Father; to him be glory and dominion for ever and ever. Amen. - Revelation 1:5,6

Another term we will use to describe this family is a Kingdom of priests. While a king denotes authority, a priest denotes ministry. This results in a ministry backed by authority! As kings, we war by ridding the earth of every giant that opposes Christ's Kingdom. As priests, we worship by filling the earth with the environment of Heaven. As a priest we have power with God in the Heavens, and as a king we have power with man in the earth. We'll never have power and favor with man in the earth if we do not have power and favor with God in the Heavens. As a priest, we experience God as worshipers and as kings we demonstrate God as warriors. It is the will of Father God to reestablish His Kingdom on planet earth through His kings and priests. The Kingdom is a realm of the authority of the King. It is the royal power, kingship, law, dominion, and territory subject to the King's rule; this is God's royal domain in the earth.

> *But if I cast out devils by the Spirit of God, then the kingdom of God is come unto you. - Matthew 12:28*

> *And as ye go, preach, saying, The kingdom of heaven is at hand. Heal the sick, cleanse the lepers, raise the dead, cast out devils: freely ye have received, freely give. - Matthew 10:7-8.*

The Kingdom of God is demonstrated in power. Without His power being demonstrated, the Kingdom has not yet come. There is no better answer to unbelief than a flow of signs, wonders, and miracles in Christ's Kingdom.

> *And he went into the synagogue, and spake boldly for*

the space of three months, disputing and persuading the things concerning the kingdom of God. - Acts 19:8

When we preach and demonstrate the Kingdom, men are persuaded of Jesus.

In our priestly ministry we introduce the Kingdom of God to mankind, which is full of salvation, healing, love, joy, peace, righteousness, wealth, and a supernatural life flowing with signs and wonders. With our kingly ministry, we rule and reign over all our enemies and circumstances, delivering creation from its present bondage and corruption.

IT IS OUT OF OUR PRIESTLY MINISTRY THAT WE FLOW IN OUR KINGLY ANOINTING!

Ministering as priests, we have compassion on the blind, the bound, the beggar, the broken and the bruised. But as His kings we have the power to deliver, heal and restore. Moreover, it

is out of our priestly ministry that we flow in our kingly anointing! As we minister to God as priests, we can move in the Spirit and His power to minister to mankind.

And he said, Thy name shall be called no more Jacob,

but Israel: for as a prince hast thou power with God and with men, and hast prevailed. - Genesis 32:28

So shalt thou find favour and good understanding in the sight of God and man. - Proverbs 3:4

As priests we find favor with God and as kings we obtain favor with men. In this present season our anointing as kings and priests brings the earthly realm under the dominion of God's Kingdom. As a priest and king, we are called to be WORSHIPING WARRIORS in this new day that has dawned upon the church.

Among many people in marketplace ministries, a present fallacy has divided kings from priests by segregation of kings and priests. They incorrectly regulate priests to the local church and the kings to the marketplace. This is not true; we are told expressively in John's Revelation that we are kings AND priests unto our God. Our priestly anointing rules the heavens so that we can wield our kingly anointing to rule in the earth. As priests, our praise, worship, and prayers open the Heavens so we can function as kings of the earth. We see this in the life of Jesus, our pattern Son.

Now when all the people were baptized, it came to pass, that Jesus also being baptized, and praying, the heaven was opened. - Luke 3:21

Our merciful High Priest, Jesus Christ, prayed and opened the Heavens with His prayers, so He could rule and reign as the King on earth. As a priest, we experience God; as kings we reveal Him in the earth.

To review, the First Reformation revealed the priesthood of every believer that granted access to God, while the Second Reformation established our prophetic ministry to mankind as oracles of our Heavenly Father. And in this final Third Reformation we receive a revelation of our kingly ministry that will infiltrate every sector of society with God's Kingdom as we reign in His stead.

There is a calling on every five-fold minister to empower the church with the KINGMAKER ANOINTING. Many are called, but few choose to move into their kingly and priestly dual anointing. A true king is a king in every circumstance, not subservient to his circumstances; instead, his circumstances serve him. To accomplish this, we need the power of the Holy Ghost, the Governor of our Heavenly Father's Kingdom.

As Governor of the Kingdom, the Holy Ghost lives within each and every one of us.

> *What? know ye not that your body is the temple of the Holy Ghost which is in you, which ye have of God, and ye are not your own? - 1 Corinthians 6:19*

> *For the kingdom is the Lord's: and he is the governor among the nations. - Psalms 22:28*

In His role as Governor, He empowers the citizens of the Kingdom of Heaven.

> *But ye shall receive power, after that the Holy Ghost is come upon you: and ye shall be witnesses unto me both in Jerusalem, and in all Judaea, and in Samaria, and unto the uttermost part of the earth. - Acts 1:8*

As the Holy Spirit governs the Father's Kingdom here on the planet, His intention is to impart the King's nature and ministry to every royal son of the Kingdom.

> *And thou Bethlehem, in the land of Juda, art not the least among the princes of Juda: for out of thee shall come a Governor, that shall rule my people Israel. - Matthew 2:6*

The nature of the King equates to the fruit of the Spirit, while the ministry of the King parallels the gifts of the Spirit.

> *But the fruit of the Spirit is love, joy, peace, longsuffering, gentleness, goodness, faith, Meekness, temperance: against such there is no law. - Galatians 6:22,23*

> *But the manifestation of the Spirit is given to every man to profit withal. For to one is given by the Spirit the word of wisdom; to another the word of knowledge by the same Spirit; To another faith by the same Spirit; to another the gifts of healing by the same Spirit; To another the working of miracles; to another prophecy; to another discerning of spirits; to another divers kinds of tongues; to another the interpretation of tongues. - 1 Corinthians 12:7-10*

The law of God's Kingdom is love. Can you imagine a world that is ruled by Kingdom love? Where this Kingdom law prevails, there is no need of any other. Such love rules over discrimination and every prejudice known to mankind. Such love eradicates every evil that dominates our world. The Governor of God's Kingdom distributes the gifts of the Spirit as He wills to His kings; these gifts are the ministry of a king. The fruit of the Spirit balances Kingdom character with the gifts of the Spirit that exercise the authority of the Kingdom.

Without this Holy Spirit anointing oil, we can't fight sickness; we need the oil. We can't flee temptation without the oil. We can't run Kingdom businesses without the oil or transform atmospheres—we need the oil. Without it, can't fight demonic giants or ever deliver creation out of its present state. The restoration of our kingly anointing is the answer to our present calamities.

Then shall the King say unto them on his right hand, Come, ye blessed of my Father, inherit the kingdom prepared for you from the foundation of the world. - Matthew 25:34

We must take back rulership and dominion over the earth because the Kingdom of God belongs to us. The majority of our problems occur because we don't take control of our circumstances. Our lives are controlled by people we hardly even know such as our banker, our employer, our doctor, government officials and the list goes on. Stress comes into our life because of our physical health, or maybe we can't pay our bills, children might be running from God, we're facing unemployment, and the list goes on. Jesus came to restore dominion back to us through the Holy Ghost with the role as Kingdom Governor to give us dominion over our circumstances. Jesus came to earth as a king to show us how He dominated circumstances. You are not meant to be a victim of your circumstances, rather they are a victim to you since the Greater One dwells in you.

God's Kingdom is about living the surrendered life as the Holy Spirit's anointing empowers us to live godly lives in this present world. The Holy Spirit does not come to give you a better life, but a new life as a new creation in Christ Jesus. The Kingdom of God does not come with observation, of us observing rules and regulations. The Kingdom resides within you right now. You are the temple of God where the Governor of the Kingdom resides within you; therefore, that makes you the Governor's mansion.

> *Let not your heart be troubled: ye believe in God, believe also in me. In my Father's house are many mansions: if it were not so, I would have told you. I go to prepare a place for you. And if I go and prepare a place for you, I will come again, and receive you unto myself; that where I am, there ye may be also. Jesus answered and said unto him, If a man love me, he will keep my words:*

and my Father will love him, and we will come unto him, and make our abode with him. But the Comforter, which is the Holy Ghost, whom the Father will send in my name, he shall teach you all things, and bring all things to your remembrance, whatsoever I have said unto you. - John 14:1-3, 23, 26

The Father's house is not a mansion over the hilltop in Heaven, as we were taught through our songbook theology. The word mansion and abode are the same Greek word "monay." The house that the Lord mentions here is not a literal house where the saints move into in the sweet by and by. No, you are the Father's mansion! We are the place of our Father's presence. In verse 23 we see that this chapter has nothing to do with going to Heaven to live in a mansion. But Heaven is coming to live and take up residence within you. Jesus said that We (Father, Son and Holy Ghost) will come into him and make our abode with him. With abode and mansion used as the same Greek word, He is literally saying, "We will mansion him." It's not about you leaving here, but about His coming here. The season has nothing to do with the disappearing of the Saints, but the appearing of the Lord. He promises "I won't leave you comfortless," denoting that He won't leave you as orphans. Adam lost fellowship with the Father and His presence. Therefore, he became an orphan. But Jesus came to restore what Adam had lost and to deliver us from the orphan spirit by making us sons in His royal Kingdom. Your covenantal reality is that the Holy Spirit lives in you. We're not to be led by rules and regulations, but by the Governor, the Holy Spirit, residing in you and me. God planted Himself in us at our new birth, impregnated us with God and we are born again of an incorruptible seed. Not only are you seated in Christ, but Christ is seated in you. Christ in you is the hope of glory, but Christ out of you is the glory; this is a present tense reality. Jesus taught us to pray these words, "For thine is the Kingdom, the power and the glory forever amen." The Kingdom is the answer, the power is the authority, and the glory is the manifest presence of God in and through the sons of God who are His kings.

Chapter 7

The Presence Driven Life

Presently, the arising kings in God's Kingdom will be known as a presence driven people. In the last season it was about the purpose driven life, which is wonderful; books have been written about a purposeful life, but now the season has changed. In fact, we may have put the cart before the horse because many have made an idol out of their purpose by replacing the presence of God in their lives focused on being purpose driven.

> *I know thy works, and thy labour, and thy patience, and how thou canst not bear them which are evil: and thou hast tried them which say they are apostles, and are not, and hast found them liars: And hast borne, and hast*

patience, and for my name's sake hast laboured, and hast not fainted. Nevertheless, I have somewhat against thee, because thou hast left thy first love. Remember therefore from whence thou art fallen, and repent, and do the first works; or else I will come unto thee quickly, and will remove thy candlestick out of his place, except thou repent. - Revelation 2:2-5

In this Scripture, Jesus commended the church at Ephesus for her great works (purpose driven), but then he delivered a rebuke because she had lost her first love (presence driven). Everything in Christ's Kingdom must have a balance. Presence is greater than purpose.

The coming moves of the Spirit will require more than faith and hope. These moves will demand something greater than what you can believe for and what you can expect. While faith and expectation are very important in our arsenal, there is yet another realm. To demonstrate this realm, we will use the Tabernacle of Moses. In the Outer Court, we grow in faith in the first realm in God. As we move into The Holy Place, we continue to grow in hope, vision and our purpose while developing our expectations in God. But we don't stop there in God. From there we move into The Most Holy Place as a third day people in the realm of intimacy with God, cultivating a presence driven life.

And now abideth faith, hope, charity, these three; but the greatest of these is charity. - 1 Corinthians 13:13

Here we see that the greatest of these three is love.

Moses is a picture of this presence driven life, representing a people who enter a deeper, intimate, and personal relationship with God. Moses was a forerunner, a prefigure of a presence driven generation. His addiction to God's presence was so great that he said, "Lord, I will not go where You are not." In essence, He was saying, I don't want to be without you, Lord. I believe Moses' greatest fear was not being able to hang out with God. Moses was known as a man that went after God. Only a few individuals were known as God's friend in the Old Testament, and Moses was one of those that God called His friend. Moses just liked to hang out with Jehovah so much so that the Israelites would ask, "Where is Moses?" And lo-and-behold, he was with God once again, disappearing for days on end. Moses and God would go on these 40-day vacations together. So intense were their discussions that it left no time to even eat or drink! One day, they both went for a walk and Moses never returned.

> *And he said, My presence shall go with thee, and I will give thee rest. And he said unto him, If thy presence go not with me, carry us not up hence. For wherein shall it be known here that I and thy people have found grace in thy sight? Is it not in that thou goest with us? So shall we be separated, I and thy people, from all the people that are upon the face of the earth. - Exodus 33:14-16*

What separated Moses from all the other people was one thing: God's presence! Accordingly, what makes us different today? God's presence. It is the distinguishing factor that sets us apart from the world and from religious people. Being a Christian alone does not set you apart; sanctification does. Setting ourselves apart in His presence makes us a different breed of believers. The kings that are coming on the scene in this day will be known for their addiction to the presence of God.

These emerging kings are called to be both a bride and a son. Brideship is intimacy with God that prepares us for sonship; sonship demonstrates God in our world. Separation defines the bride, while demonstration defines a son. You must first relate to Him in brideship, which is a presence driven life, for without it you will never move into sonship to demonstrate and manifest Christ. Our brideship predicates our sonship. To mature as a son, you must be His bride, so in love with our heavenly bridegroom, Jesus.

And the Lord spake unto Moses face to face, as a man speaketh unto his friend. And he turned again into the camp: but his servant Joshua, the son of Nun, a young man, departed not out of the tabernacle. - Exodus 33:11

I believe Joshua became Moses' successor for one reason: his same addiction to God's presence. He would linger in His presence long after Moses went home. There was no better candidate to lead the people of God than a presence driven man like Joshua.

During the days of Moses and David, the Lord left the Heavens to come and live in a box called the Ark, so He could be close to these two men. Now that's extreme! The Lord longs to be with you and me in the same manner. For example, to keep my wife, I had to go to extremes by changing my lifestyle, including cutting off my old friends and making major sacrifices. It cost me everything to get married to my beautiful wife. So it is with our relationship with God; it will cost us everything. What extremes have you taken to be a presence driven person? In the church, there are too many therapies and formulas for the people of God. We have rehabilitation programs and seven-step programs for those who have serious addictions, which, in the end, help maybe a few people. But I have a one step program: get addicted to Jesus!

YOU CANNOT BE IN HIS PRESENCE WITHOUT IT BECOMING VISIBLE IN YOUR LIFE.

And ye shall seek me, and find me, when ye shall search for me with all your heart. And I will be found of you,

saith the Lord: and I will turn away your captivity, and I will gather you from all the nations, and from all the places whither I have driven you, saith the Lord; and I will bring you again into the place whence I caused you to be carried away captive. - Jeremiah 29:13,14

The Lord told David, "If you go to heaven, I'll find you there. If you make your bed in hell, I'll chase you there also." Notice the pursuit of God's love for David. The Lord has that same love for us. May we in return have that same pursuit for the presence of God so that wherever He is, we desire to be with Him. Think about this: Jesus Christ told His apostles, "I'll never leave you or forsake you." He longed to be with them and never leave them. His disciples were known as the people of His presence in the book of Acts. People saw them and knew that they had been with Jesus.

Now when they saw the boldness of Peter and John, and perceived that they were unlearned and ignorant men, they marvelled; and they took knowledge of them, that they had been with Jesus. - Acts 4:13

I want it to be apparent to the world that Mark Kauffman has been with Jesus. Jesus wants to hang out with you. In fact, He thinks you are really cool, and the invitation has gone out to all, "And whosoever will, let him come."

And when he had removed him, he raised up unto them David to be their king; to whom also he gave their testimony, and said, I have found David the son of Jesse, a man after mine own heart, which shall fulfil all my will. - Acts 13:22

What made David different? He was a man after God's own heart. I say it this way; he was a man after God! He loved the presence of God. When King Saul found himself in trouble, he feared he was going to lose his throne. But compare when David faced trouble; he was solely afraid of losing the presence of God. What a difference between these two!

Create in me a clean heart, O God; and renew a right spirit within me. Cast me not away from thy presence; and take not thy holy spirit from me. - Psalms 51:10,11

Moses spent so much time with the Lord that his face shined. Israel beheld God's face in the face of Moses. Oh, that we too would radiate the presence of God so much that people would see Him shine in and through us. You cannot be in His presence without it becoming visible in your life. The world needs to see the evidence of His presence on the people of God.

And there were certain Greeks among them that came up to worship at the feast: The same came therefore to Philip, which was of Bethsaida of Galilee, and desired him, saying, Sir, we would see Jesus. Philip cometh and telleth Andrew and again Andrew and Philip tell Jesus. And Jesus answered them, saying, The hour is come, that the Son of man should be glorified. Verily, verily,

I say unto you, Except a corn of wheat fall into the ground and die, it abideth alone: but if it die, it bringeth forth much fruit. He that loveth his life shall lose it; and he that hateth his life in this world shall keep it unto life eternal. If any man serve me, let him follow me; and where I am, there shall also my servant be: if any man serve me, him will my Father honour. Now is my soul troubled; and what shall I say? Father, save me from this hour: but for this cause came I unto this hour.
- John 12:20-27

The Greeks said to Philip, "Sir, we will see Jesus." So Philip told Andrew and then they went to Jesus who responded, "Except a corn of wheat fall in the ground and die, it abides alone but if it dies, it will bring forth much fruit." I always thought this a strange response to their question, but one day the Holy Spirit shed light on this passage of Scripture. During His life, Jesus was the single, solitary individual on the face of the earth to possess eternal life, the Holy Spirit and the Father's nature. He was the head but lacked a body.

And Jesus saith unto him, The foxes have holes, and the birds of the air have nests; but the Son of man hath not where to lay his head. - Matthew 8:20

This verse in the Gospel of Matthew does not mean that Jesus lacked a place to sleep. In this statement, Jesus explained that He was the head, but had nobody to place his head on. Until the day of Pentecost in Acts 2, He had nowhere to lay His head. Being confined to a human body, He only could be in one place at one time. Thus, Jesus resembled the corn of wheat that would fall into the ground and die, so that He could reproduce himself in us via the Holy Ghost.

> *Nevertheless, I tell you the truth; It is expedient for you that I go away: for if I go not away, the Comforter will not come unto you; but if I depart, I will send him unto you. - John 16:7*

Jesus was telling His disciples He must depart so He could impart Himself into them.

> *Even the Spirit of truth; whom the world cannot receive, because it seeth him not, neither knoweth him: but ye know him; for he dwelleth with you, and shall be in you. - John 14:17*

In this passage, He tells them how they will soon become a people of His presence.

> *Father, glorify thy name. Then came there a voice from heaven, saying, I have both glorified it, and will glorify it again. - John 12:28*

Then, when Jesus asked the Father to glorify His name, a voice came from Heaven saying, "I have glorified it and I will glorify it again." The Father glorified His name in Jesus Christ, the head of the church, and now once again, in this Kingdom season, He will glorify His name in and through His body, the church, the sons of God, His emerging kings. God is about to do it again! He will glorify Himself in the sons of God—what a glorious day to be alive!

Behold, he cometh with clouds; and every eye shall see him, and they also which pierced him: and all kindreds of the earth shall wail because of him. Even so, Amen.
- Revelation 1:7

As a young boy, I thought this verse would be fulfilled by every eye seeing Jesus on television. But no, that's not what He meant. Every eye will see Him in you and me; isn't this glorious? The Greeks said, "Sir, we would see Jesus." Saints of the Most High God, it is the Father's greatest desire that the world would see Jesus in you and me. Let's not just tell the world about Jesus, let's show them Jesus. It's show and tell time!

God is begging to become visible in the earth in and through His body, the church. It must be tangible! Jesus said, "The Spirit of the Lord is upon Me," indicating that the anointing was visible and very tangible upon Him. Jesus was born with the Spirit of God, but when He said the "Spirit of the Lord is upon Me," all that which was hidden in Him for 30 years would now be unveiled and made visible upon Him for all the world to see. His kingly anointing would now be revealed during His 3 ½ year ministry. Jesus experienced an epiphany with the Spirit of God. Epiphany comes from two Greek words: Epi meaning upon and phanaroo meaning apparent, to manifest. What has always been apparent to God is about to become apparent to you and others in this Kingdom season. What He has always known about you will be made known to you and everyone in your world. There's so much more to you than what meets the eye. We are living in a season of epiphanies. It's apparent to Heaven first, then it appears on the natural plain. Your eye has not seen, your ear has not heard, neither has it entered your heart that which God has already prepared for you in heavenly places in Christ Jesus. Everyone around will see you as God sees you. The first time I saw my wife, I had an epiphany. I fell in love immediately, and suddenly, I knew she would be my bride. Now that's an epiphany. They come suddenly, swiftly, quickly, immediately, and they are coming now.

An epiphany is when Jesus steps into your boat. Think about the disciples that had been toiling all night, battling the contradicting winds. They were only 6 miles from one side of the shore and on their way to the other when suddenly Jesus stepped into their boat, and immediately, they were on the shore. Some of you presently are toiling in your ministry, with your finances, in business, battling in your health, struggling with family issues, and in your marriage. But once Jesus steps in, suddenly the storm will cease. Stay in the boat, He is coming. Don't be so busy toiling that you miss the presence of God right before you. When He steps in, suddenly you're in your destiny. Suddenly He appears, suddenly the vision becomes a reality, suddenly the dream comes to pass, and suddenly the storm will cease. Anything can happen now in this season of epiphanies.

> *And we know all things work together for good to them that love God, to them who are the called according to his purpose. - Romans 8:28*

This is not a generic statement; it's a reality—a promise that you can hold on to when contradicting circumstances have come against you.

This is a season of epiphanies, when the Spirit of God comes upon you tangibly, visibly by manifesting in and through you. As an apocalypse, it uncovers and unveils the Christ within you. Christ in you is the hope of glory, but Christ coming out of you is the glory.

> *For the earnest expectation of the creature waiteth for the manifestation of the sons of God. - Romans 8:19*

Creation is not waiting for a revelation, but a manifestation of God's love in and through the sons of God. We are not called to only tell the world we love them; we must show them. I want the presence of God to ooze out of your pores. What will set you apart from the world is His presence, like the early church, who were known as the people of His presence. Let the kings arise, and forever be known as a presence driven people.

> *Howbeit when he, the Spirit of truth, is come, he will guide you into all truth: for he shall not speak of himself; but whatsoever he shall hear, that shall he speak: and he will shew you things to come. He shall glorify me:*

for he shall receive of mine, and shall shew it unto you. All things that the Father hath are mine: therefore said I, that he shall take of mine, and shall shew it unto you.
- John 16:13-15

In this passage, the Lord unmasks the evidence of God's presence in a person's life. Here are the six characteristics that Jesus said the Holy Spirit manifests to you and through you to display the evidence of a presence driven life:

1. You will receive a revelation of truth of who you are as a king, priest, and prophet.
2. The Spirit of God will empower you to see your future, and as a prophetic person, you will see things to come.
3. You will have an ear to hear the voice of your Heavenly Father.
4. Your life will glorify your Heavenly Father.
5. You will experience the supernatural dimension.
6. The Spirit of God doesn't just want to use you, but to dwell in you as His habitation.

There could be nothing more miserable than losing the presence of God. Samson's life is tragic because he lost the presence of God. You can be saved, going to Heaven, and escape hell, but still lose His presence in your life. Samson overcame many of Israel's enemies, yet failed to defeat his own personal sins. You may help others, but still neglect to help yourself. Sin must be conquered and dealt with if we want God's presence. Do you know that sin cannot stay in your life except if you grant it permission?

> And I say also unto thee, That thou art Peter, and upon this rock I will build my church; and the gates of hell shall not prevail against it. And I will give unto thee the keys of the kingdom of heaven: and whatsoever thou shalt bind on earth shall be bound in heaven: and whatsoever thou shalt loose on earth shall be loosed in heaven. - Matthew 16:18-19

Hell's goal is to allure you into sin, away from God's presence. Whatever you permit will be permitted and whatever you don't permit will not be permitted. Choose well. Because of lukewarmness, lethargy, and laziness, men lose their first love for Jesus.

> Thou shalt have no other gods before me. - Exodus 20:3

> All that ever came before me are thieves and robbers: but the sheep did not hear them. - John 10:8

Anything you put before Christ and His Kingdom, whether it be your work, family, hobbies, or other relationships, will steal His Presence from you. Jehovah said we are to have no other gods before Him and Jesus said whatever comes before Him is but a thief and robber. Anything that you put before God is a thief and it robs you of His presence. I've learned to be rude to hell and all its temptations. You can't whisper to hell to get out of your life; you must be ruthless and very rude.

Samson lost an incredible thing in his life: the presence of God. Do you remember when he killed a young lion? Days after, he came back to the dead carcass that had honey inside, and he ate it. Hell tastes sweet when you partake of it, but it's sour to the stomach the very next day. Let's look at the example of anger. Anger is manipulation to get people to back off. It may initially taste sweet when people back down, but the next day it will be bitter to your stomach. We must avoid the Samson syndrome and rise as kings by taking dominion to deal with all our enemies, including whatever sins, weaknesses, idiosyncrasies and shortcomings involved. All anger, jealousy, a bad temper, and uncontrolled addictions must go. The Holy Spirit needs your cooperation to overcome your weaknesses for you to be presence driven men and women. Our strength is not in our confession alone, but in our possession of His presence. Our victory comes by confessions backed by His presence. Our strength is in our covenant with the Lord. Samson had great gifts and was used by the Lord, but never understood the indwelling presence of God. The Holy Ghost comes to conquer and rule every area of our lives if we permit Him to do so. What did Samson love? Samson loved Samson. It's evident he had no deep love for God, neither did he call on Him; he never built God an altar. We never see him praying to God, like Noah, Abraham, Moses, Joshua, Gideon, David, or Solomon. Even Samson's own parents built an altar to the Lord. It amazes me how men that have committed adultery still have power to uproot the powers of darkness in other people's lives. This is hard to understand, but the gifts and callings of God are without repentance, they are irrevocable, and God will never take a gift from you.

Samson loved Delilah most of all. Delilah had a seducing spirit; these spirits come to find your weaknesses. If they can steal your strength by attacking your weak areas, they rob you of a presence driven life. Since Samson died with his enemies, he failed to conquer them. You can succeed in life, business, ministry, but absolutely fail in character. Please stay out of polluted waters. God has invested too much in you.

> *Now unto him that is able to keep you from falling, and to present you faultless before the presence of his glory with exceeding joy. - Jude 1:24*

God not only saves, delivers, and heals us, but He also keeps us. Personally, He kept me from religion so I would not be polluted by false teachings. He will do everything to keep us from falling into any temptation. We all should make Matthew 6:12 part of our daily prayer: "lead us not into temptation but deliver us from evil." Samson dealt with uncontrollable appetites, but he never fled them. We must flee temptation. Flee is a running word. When Delilah had cut off his hair (a type of his covenant with God), Samson was cut off from the presence of God. Self-indulgence was Samson's main problem, and we must recognize and overcome this enemy if we are to be a presence driven people.

Delilah came to find the source of Samson's strength. Hell is after whatever is the source of our strength. I'm talking to leaders now as well; if you're a leader and can't apply the Word to yourself, you'll find yourself in serious trouble. The spirit of Delilah is roaming the land in these days, seeking whom it may devour. This spirit affects both men and women; when you entertain it, it will lull you to sleep. Sleeping saints become comfortable in the lap of Delilah. It's time for everyone to wake up the king inside of you and resist laying your head in the lap of this spirit. Instead, rise to overcome all of our enemies. The spirit of Delilah is very subtle and sneaky, for little by little she draws you into her web. How do I know someone has fallen into a spiritual slumber? They can go 30 days without praying. When prayer has lost its place in their life, they now make decisions without God. They slide on their tithes and offerings, becoming thieves and robbers. Your tithe has nothing to do with money, but the position God has in your heart. I was taught to tithe from the time I was a young boy. I learned the importance of tithing and how it connected me with God. I've taught my son, Christian Mark, the principles of tithing and he has been faithful with his tithes as well. You will only teach your children what's valuable to you because where your treasure is, your heart is also. If the Lord has your heart, He will also have your tithe.

Delilah shaved Samson's head, and he awakened to bondage. His hair was a sign of God's covenant with Samson and, with its loss, the Spirit of God departed his life. I can live my life and lose my stuff, but I can't afford to live my life and lose the presence of God. Then Samson's eyes were gouged out by his enemies, blinding him. If we follow the path of Samson, we will become spiritually blind and lose our vision. Without holiness, no one can see. They tied him to a millstone, a place where the ox would grind out the grain. Now he was serving his enemies' purposes instead of the Lord's. Let's magnify the Lord and not our enemies. The latest figures say that 90% of boys and 60% of girls from the age of 13 to 19 have been exposed to pornography. Another figure says 54% of born again Christians view porn at least once a month. When men and women view these evil images, they tread down the enemy's seeds and feed this giant demon called lust. Samson walked in circles, treading on the grain. Carnality will feed and magnify your enemies, instead of glorifying God. Samson's enemies asked him, "Where is your God now?" That is a grief-stricken question, and I don't want that testimony about my life.

And Samson said unto the lad that held him by the hand, Suffer me that I may feel the pillars whereupon the house standeth, that I may lean upon them. - Judges 16:26

A little child showed up to help Samson. The prophet of old said "a child shall lead them." Do we have to wait for the next generation to bring deliverance to creation? I pray not!

> *And Samson said, Let me die with the Philistines. And he bowed himself with all his might; and the house fell upon the lords, and upon all the people that were therein. So the dead which he slew at his death were more than they which he slew in his life. - Judges 16:30*

Samson broke covenant, yet God strengthened him one more time. Our God cannot break covenant with you and me. He will do everything to destroy our enemies.

It's decision time—will you have a presence driven life or a life without His presence? The worst thing that could ever happen to you is for God to ignore you. People want God to touch them, but they never want to touch God. Our strength and power only come through a presence driven life. He must be more than the Lord; He must be my Lord. The Scriptures call Him the great shepherd, the good shepherd, the chief shepherd, but I love what David called Him, "The Lord is my shepherd." He made the Lord his possession, revealing the level of intimacy he had with Him. Don't be like Samson, who lived too comfortably in the enemy's territory.

COMPARING DAVID AND SAMSON

DAVID	SAMSON
Presence driven	Purpose driven
Killed a Philistine	Married a Philistine
Moved in revelation	Moved in inspiration
Overcame for God's glory	Overcame for his own glory
Operated within a team	Operated independently
Left a legacy	Left no legacy
Strength in the Name of the Lord	Strength in his hair
Integrity of the Lord	No integrity
Fulfilled his purpose	Never fulfilled his purpose

Although Samson's name means discernment, he couldn't discern right from wrong. Real power is internal, flowing out of a consecrated life of purity. It comes out of passion and pursuit for King Jesus based on the degree that you love Him. It's not about the power of God, but knowing the God of power. The Lord is going to have a people of His presence even now, as we are moving from gifts to presence. Samson had gifting and power, but no presence in his life. The story of Sampson reveals how the spirit of Delilah can rob you of your intimacy and power. Power is found in an intimate relationship with Jesus Christ. Hell's commitment to our destruction seems greater than our desire to destroy hell. Hell seems to be more committed to making people sick than we are to healing them. Hell seems to be more committed to populating hell than we are populating the Kingdom of Heaven. This must change and it will change when Christ's kings arise and become presence driven. As these kings arise, they will put all their enemies under their feet.

You can learn more about the presence driven life in my book entitled *The Presence Driven Leader*.

DR. MARK KAUFFMAN

Chapter 8

Restored Image

And God said, Let us make man in our image, after our likeness: and let them have dominion over the fish of the sea, and over the fowl of the air, and over the cattle, and over all the earth, and over every creeping thing that creepeth upon the earth. So God created man in his own image, in the image of God created he him; male and female created he them. And God blessed them, and God said unto them, Be fruitful, and multiply, and replenish the earth, and subdue it: and have dominion over the fish of the sea, and over the fowl of the air, and over every living thing that moveth upon the earth. - Genesis 1:26-28

This passage of scripture reveals God's original purpose and intent for mankind: to bear the image of God and have dominion in the earth. This was mankind's original assignment and in this passage, we see that bearing His image comes before dominion. Presently, the church is seeking power without restoring the proper image back to its people. I don't look for dominion from without, it's locked up within the image of Christ inside of me. Dominion flows out of our identity and state of being in Christ. The reason the church has lost its power is that it has lost the image of God. Jesus' mission statement was to restore "that" which was lost. "That" is the image of God and dominion returned to us in the earth. Let me make this clear: restoring the image of God and establishing our dominion on the planet was the plan of redemption. Redemption was not to save you so you could go to Heaven someday. When God restores your true image, then and only then will He restore dominion as well. The word dominion derives from the word authority or to rule. A ruler is a standard which you measure things. A king is a ruler by which others have a standard. As kings in Christ's Kingdom, we are to become the rule that sets the standard for creation. As we look to King Jesus, who is the model King, we become that standard. You and I were born into a royal family of kings to rule and reign in our world.

The law of the Lord is perfect, converting the soul: the testimony of the Lord is sure, making wise the simple.
- Psalms 19:7

Convert is a powerful word; in the Greek, it means restoring back and to bring back home again. Most Christians are not converts. Now don't throw this book away because I made that statement. I grew up hearing preachers say when someone gave their life to Jesus, "We have a new convert today." That is not biblical, and to be honest with you, I have not met many converts in my life. So then, who is really converted? When you're converted, the law of the Lord is perfected in your mind, returning you back to the state that man was in before the fall–back to a state of fellowship, dominion, intimacy, and kingship in Christ Jesus. This is restored identity and true conversion. Conversion is a process NOT an event. The word law means doctrine. Through apostolic doctrine and truth, He restores us and gives us a true conversion.

We are only converted when we are in dominion!

From whence come wars and fightings among you? Come they not hence, even of your lusts that war in your members? - James 4:1

The church of Jesus Christ at large has a serious identity crisis. While the church condemns the world because of their confusion with identity, I truly believe that there is confusion out in the world because there's confusion in the church. When the church comes into her true identity, then and only then can we bring the world into their true identity. Sin can be defined as a mistaken identity. When you and I sin and fall short of the mark, it's because we just forgot who we were in Christ. Mistaken identities have paralyzed the church and hijacked us out of the truth of who we really are in Christ. I wrote this book to introduce you to the real you. You were born into royalty, as a new creation, a king and priest of the Most High God. The King and His Kingdom are already resident within you right now!

> *And when he was demanded of the Pharisees, when the kingdom of God should come, he answered them and said, the kingdom of God cometh not with observation: Neither shall they say, Lo here! Or, lo there! For, behold, the kingdom of God is within you. - Luke 17:20,21*

Jesus said, "out of the midst of your belly will flow rivers of living water." Everything flows out of your image and true state of being in Christ. Therefore, a new convert is not one who asked Jesus into his life, but a saint who has recovered their true identity in Christ and is walking in dominion.

> *For if any be a hearer of the word, and not a doer, he is like unto a man beholding his natural face in a glass: For he beholdeth himself, and goeth his way, and straightway forgetteth what manner of man he was. - James 1:23-24*

The Word of God is a mirror: it reveals who you are, what you have and what you can do in Christ. I was raised in churches where I was told what I couldn't do, but the Bible reveals not only what we should not do, but it tells us what we can do in Christ.

I can do all things through Christ which strengtheneth me. - Philippians 4:13.

The Bible is the operator's manual for the emerging kings and priests in the earth. God's Word does not condemn us for our weaknesses, nor is it given to us to become better humans. The Bible is a manual for our new creation reality. You are a new creation being that has the DNA of your Heavenly Father; your Father's genes are in you right now. Possessing our Father's genes, we can grow into the nature of our Father (the fruit of the Spirit) and we can grow into the ministry of our Lord (the gifts of the Spirit). We are in Christ and Christ is in us; we have the best of both worlds. Paul told the church of Corinth they were acting like mere men, forgetting who they were in Christ. The American church is much like the church at Corinth, in that they have forgotten who they are. We have entered a time and season that we must recover our true identity. Jesus' death, burial and resurrection was to make you new, not just good. Jesus did not come to make you a better person, but to make you a new creation, a rare species.

> *By his own wish, he made us his own sons through the Word of truth that we might be, so to speak, the first specimens of his new creation. - James 1:18 J.B. Phillips Translation*

Jesus did not come to give you a better life, but to give you a brand-new life as a new creation. He didn't come to improve your life, but to transform your life to resemble Himself as the pattern, son Jesus. When the church recaptures the revelation of their kingship, they will become the most powerful force world has ever seen.

Death and life are in the power of the tongue: and they that love it shall eat the fruit thereof. - Proverbs 18:21

We must be careful of the words that we speak for they either release us or restrict us.

For by thy words thou shalt be justified, and by thy words thou shalt be condemned. - Matthew 12:37

Our own words will bind us, or they will free us. The Lord told Jeremiah that he was called to be a prophet and he responded with, "I am just a child." The Lord rebuked him by saying, "Don't you ever say that again!" Why? Like a train track, words go before us until we move into the experience or the reality of those words. So many people try to find out who they are by turning to others who don't even know who they are and who live out of a mistaken identity. If a person is confused about their gender, they shouldn't go to someone else who is also confused about their gender to find answers. They should go to the One who created them, Who knows what He made them: male or female. If I don't understand the meaning of a painting, I will go to the painter to tell me what the painting means. My wife and I own the second oldest flower shop in America. I've been a floral designer for over 40 years. Now, you can tell me that one of my designs is a cat, but it doesn't change the fact that it's a flower bouquet. As the designer of that bouquet, I know why I created it the way I did. If everyone who is confused about their personal identity would go back to their Maker and believe in the original purpose and intent why He made them, then all the confusion would go away.

Our universities are filled with students changing their majors and that's just another result of a mistaken identity. My son is preparing to go to Duquesne University this year as a freshman. He will not be changing his major in the coming years because he knows why God created him, why he's in the earth and what he's called to do. You cannot tell an architect the house they designed and built is a boat. Likewise, you can't tell the Creator you are a woman if you're a man, for He designed you to either be male or female. God is not confused; He did not make a mistake. If you are confused about who you are, make sure you go to someone who is not confused about their identity and who understands why God created them. Even many pastors are confused with their identity, so they continually call the saints of God sinners. You and I were sinners, but we have been washed in the blood of Jesus, saved by His grace, and now have become saints. The Apostle Paul did not write letters to the sinners in the churches, but in his writings, he calls them saints.

Paul, an apostle of Jesus Christ by the will of God, to

the saints which are at Ephesus, and to the faithful in Christ Jesus. - Ephesians 1:1

Jesus asked His disciples, "Who do men say I am?" After they responded, He then asked them, "Who do you say I am?" If you don't know who you are then you can't tell me who I am.

When Jesus came into the coasts of Caesarea Philippi, he asked his disciples, saying, Whom do men say that I the Son of man am? And they said, Some say that thou art John the Baptist: some, Elias; and others, Jeremias, or one of the prophets. He saith unto them, But whom say ye that I am? And Simon Peter answered and said, Thou art the Christ, the Son of the living God. And Jesus answered and said unto him, Blessed art thou, Simon Barjona: for flesh and blood hath not revealed it unto thee, but my Father which is in heaven. And I say also unto thee, That thou art Peter, and upon this rock I will build my church; and the gates of hell shall not prevail against it. And I will give unto thee the keys of the kingdom of heaven: and whatsoever thou shalt bind on earth shall be bound in heaven: and whatsoever thou shalt loose on earth shall be loosed in heaven. - Matthew 16:13-19

Everyone was confused with Jesus' identity except Jesus. Finally, Peter got the revelation! I don't care if people are confused with who I am, because I know who I am. If you are confused about who you are and people are confused about who you are, I pray you will not be confused after reading this book. Peter got a revelation of Christ and Christ gave Peter a revelation of his true identity.

It's not what others know about Christ that will cause you to stand in crisis and prevail over your enemies, it's the revelation that you have about Christ that will cause you to stand in the midst of crisis. A revelation of Christ, the healer, will keep you when your body is under attack. A revelation of Christ the provider will keep you when you lose your job or your business is struggling and you can't pay the bills. A revelation of Christ will keep you unshakable when everything is being shaken. A revelation of Christ's love will keep you when others forsake you and walk out on you. A revelation of Christ and who you are in Christ gives you access to the keys of the Kingdom and true dominion. When all hell breaks loose, it's not what others say about Christ, but what you know about Him by your revelation that will cause you to stand.

Jesus spent the rest of His life making I AM statements. If you fail to live out of I AM decrees, you'll end up living out of what people say about you. Multiple times He unmasked His true identity with I AM statements: I AM the Bread of Life, I AM the Way, the Truth and the Life, I AM the Door, I AM the Good Shepherd, I AM the True Vine, I AM the Resurrection and the Life, I AM the Light of the World. This may sound somewhat arrogant, but in truth, it's just His confidence in knowing who He was in His Father's Kingdom. Like Jesus, the righteous are to be as bold as a lion. Never be fearful of declaring who you are in Christ!

We should make it a practice of making I am statements just like Jesus did. Declare:
- I am the righteousness of God in Christ Jesus
- I am worthy to be partakers of the saints' inheritance
- I am seated with Christ in Heavenly places
- I am a king and priest after the order of Melchizedek
- I am a son of God
- I am chosen for greatness
- I am His workmanship, created in Christ unto good works,
- I am the seed of Abraham and the seed of David
- I am the bride of Christ
- I am an heir of God and joint heir with Jesus Christ
- I am saved by the blood of Jesus
- I am healed by the stripes of Jesus
- I am ambassador of Christ's Kingdom
- I am the temple of the Living God
- I am the elect and favored by my God
- I am born again of an incorruptible seed
- I am sanctified and filled with Heaven's Holy Ghost

- I am blessed with all spiritual blessings in heavenly places

The Bible says let the redeemed of the Lord say so. When you declare truth, it will make you free. You must refuse to allow other people's insecurities to reflect your identity. Their insecurities do not determine who you are; God's Word does. And never let someone else's false identity change your true identity. We cannot permit people who don't know who they are to determine who we are.

YOU MUST REFUSE TO ALLOW OTHER PEOPLE'S INSECURITIES TO REFLECT YOUR IDENTITY.

Ignorance is the greatest enemy to the church; people perish because of their lack of knowledge. I tell my congregation that you don't come to church to maintain your salvation. When we come to church, we learn how to think right and to apply the Word to our lives. We don't gather every Sunday for an emotional fix, but to exchange our minds and walk out with a renewed mind.

And be renewed in the spirit of your mind - Ephesians 4:23

The prodigal came to himself one day in a pigpen, had a revelation of his true identity and returned to his father's house as a son. Churches are filled with prodigal sons that are about to get a revelation of who they really are and awaken to their true identity and purpose. Once again, it's not what people declare you to be, it's what you say about yourself that really matters. Learn to make decrees over your own life with, I am statements.

I'm thankful for prophets, but I don't need a prophet to tell me who I am anymore because I know who I am. I've met so many people in the last 30 years who chase prophets across the country because they really do not know their identity in Christ. True prophets bring revelation and confirmation of who you really are in Christ. People want you to have a weak image of yourself, but when you have looked in the mirror of God's Word and can see who you are and what you have, their opinions become irrelevant. Everything that you have need of and will ever become is already encrypted in your spirit man. You have more than you think you have! You can do more than you think you can do! And you'll be more than you think you'll ever be! True prophetic words are not just meant to encourage people, but to reveal who they are in Christ. Truth will make you free of other's opinions of you and truth will demand a response. Give up ignorance for wisdom and truth.

I grew up in religion that told us how to behave, but it never taught us our true identity. Behavior modification comes by the law giving us the list of do's and do not's, but identity releases God's nature into our spirits, so that His nature becomes our nature. Being born in the Kingdom means I live out of Kingdom principles not because I have to, but because I want to. You don't have to teach a duck to swim or take them to swimming lessons. The duck just takes to the water naturally because he is a duck. Dogs bark because they're dogs, lions roar because they're lions, sinners sin because they are sinners, and as the sons of God, we manifest Christ because it's in our nature. Nothing could be worse than living in the planet and not knowing who you really are, why you are here and what you're called to do. Surround yourself with people who know who they are and what they have in Christ. A genuine friend is anyone who helps you get to your destiny. I meet people all the time who live in the past resulting from their failures. Never allow your failures to determine your identity.

According as he hath chosen us in him before the foundation of the world, that we should be holy and without blame before him in love. - Ephesians 1:4

Before the foundation of the world, God had a meeting about you. The Father and the Son were present, and the Holy Ghost was there taking the minutes at that meeting. God had predetermined His will for you, and you were chosen in Him before He constructed the foundation of the world. In that meeting, they determined the plan to redeem mankind should he fail after he was created.

> *And all that dwell upon the earth shall worship him, whose names are not written in the book of life of the Lamb slain from the foundation of the world. - Revelation 13:8*

The Lamb was slain from the foundation of the world, long before man fell in the garden. Satan said in the garden after he enticed Adam and Eve to sin, "Check, I got them," but God, before the foundation of the world was laid, had already declared, "Checkmate!" When you messed up last week, God didn't freak out, for He already made provision for your sins, weaknesses, and failures. Your salvation was part of the plan long before you ever needed it. Too many Christians are waiting for what God is going to do instead of getting the revelation of what God has already done. Stop waiting for the next breakthrough and get a revelation that Jesus already broke through. Let's rise and act out of what God has already done. Our faith lives out of the finished work of Jesus Christ. What you believe in is what you will act out. I work out of who I am. If you believe you're a son of God, then you'll act like a son of God. Similarly, if you believe you were born to fail, then you will probably fail. Whatever you believe you were born into, you will ultimately live out. When you were born again by the Spirit of God, you were translated out of the Adam's family and put into Christ's family. In this new family of God that you were born again into, there are no generational curses, no bloodline diseases, and no poverty in your new pedigree. Learn to live out of the new creation man that you were redeemed to become.

> *Therefore, if any man be in Christ, he is a new creature: old things are passed away; behold, all things are become new. - 2 Corinthians 5:17*

> *For the grace of God that bringeth salvation hath appeared to all men, teaching us that, denying ungodliness and worldly lusts, we should live soberly, righteously, and godly in this present world. - Titus 2:11-12*

Grace is a teacher; the grace of God teaches us to deny ungodliness and worldliness so we can live righteous lives in this present world. His grace is sufficient for you and me. Grace is what God did for us in Christ, while faith is what we do in response. Grace is not the freedom to do whatever we want to do, but it's a life force that enables us to do what is righteous and just. It is the Lord's divine empowerment. Not given to cover our imperfections, grace empowers us to obtain a victory over our imperfections. Grace enables us through the new creation man to live righteous, holy lives.

> *Wherefore, my beloved, as ye have always obeyed, not as in my presence only, but now much more in my absence, work out your own salvation with fear and trembling. - Philippians 2:12*

We don't work for our salvation, but we work out our

salvation. Grace is not just living for Him, but it's Christ living through us. Some hyper-grace preachers use it as a covering, but real grace is not just a covering but a cleansing. Grace empowers us to deny ourselves. Denying myself is not denying the living of my life here in the earth, but it is denying my fleshly works and accepting His finished work on the cross as my provision. Grace is a revelation that we can't do anything on our own. Grace is a person named Jesus Christ and without Him, we can do nothing.

I am the vine, ye are the branches: He that abideth in me, and I in him, the same bringeth forth much fruit: for without me ye can do nothing. - John 15:5

Predestined means pre-before. You were not saved to go to Heaven, but to fulfill the great plan and destiny God has for you. God has already predetermined your life from the moment that you would accept Him in your life, including the destiny He already has planned for you.

And from Jesus Christ, who is the faithful witness, and the first begotten of the dead, and the prince of the kings of the earth. Unto him that loved us, and washed us from our sins in his own blood, and hath made us kings and priests unto God and his Father; to him be glory and dominion for ever and ever. Amen. - Revelation 1:5,6

The blood of Jesus has washed you and redeemed you from your past, restoring your true identity as kings and priests in the earth. If my mother had aborted me, she would've killed an author, a businessman, an entrepreneur, an apostle, a doctor, a husband, and a father. Abortion is not just the death of a baby, but the death of a destiny.

Too many people live out of their soul realm and not out of the image of God.

For as many as are led by the Spirit of God, they are the sons of God. - Romans 8:14

We are to be led by our spirit man, not our soul man The soul is defined by our feelings and emotions. We are to be governed by Christ within us and the Word of the Lord; when we do, we will be strong in the Lord and in the power of His might. When man lives out of his soul, he creates a weak image of himself, but when he lives out of the image of God, he creates a strong image of himself. Paul said, "I am the same no matter what state I am in." Paul did not live out of his emotions and feelings, but was governed by his spirit. I can tell a lot about someone's soul by their giving, praise, commitment, servanthood, stewardship, faithfulness, loyalty, and love. Hell comes after your soul. Worry and fear reflect from your soul; therefore, you must guard and protect your soul by living out of your spirit man. Damaged souls have a hard time interpreting who they really are and who God really is to them. We must learn to live out of what God says about us and not someone else's crazy opinion of us. Every day, put on the helmet of salvation to guard your mind.

Humanly empowered Christianity has changed nothing. But a divinely empowered church alone will transform our present world. Only by the supernatural grace and power of the Holy Spirit through the church will we transform our world. Most believers don't even know what the Scriptures are intended for. They think the Bible is a standard for living and that we should attempt to live up to it, which is humanly impossible. That will never work in all our natural, feeble efforts. The Bible is not a book of rules for you to keep, but a Kingdom manual to show you your true identity in Christ and to reveal the supernatural life of Christ that dwells within you. Religion has robbed the church from walking in our new creation realities. The greatest enemy to the church has not been the devil, but religion. God planted Himself in you! New birth impregnated you with God! Hell wants you and me to live in fear of failing God and coming short of His glory. Hell wants you to believe that you're not meeting up with the standard. Your life is not based upon what you can do, but on what He has already done. We need to learn to live out of the reality of what God has said about us. We need preachers of righteousness to tell us the truth about who we are and what we have in Christ. The Apostle Paul said, "I preach nothing but Christ." He preached nothing but the new creation man.

Study to shew thyself approved unto God, a workman that needeth not to be ashamed, rightly dividing the word of truth. - 2 Timothy 2:15

When I first read this, I believe I had to study really hard so God would approve of me. Then one day the Holy Spirit shed light on this Scripture and I saw it! As I study the Scriptures, I see I am already approved in Christ because of what He has done for me. So now I study to get a revelation of my approval in Christ.

The unregenerated man is living out of the wrong image that God has for him. You were created in God's likeness and image. The Apostle Paul said, "Christ is the image of God." Therefore, Christ and His Word are God's true image of you.

For whom he did foreknow, he also did predestinate to be conformed to the image of his Son, that he might be the firstborn among many brethren. - Romans 8:29

What we behold is what we become. God is restoring His true image back into the earth through His kings and priests. Hell comes to mar that image of God in you. People have many images of themselves: a successful image, a sexy image, a macho image, an intellectual image, a bad boy image, a poor image, and a failing image. These are all poor images that God did not give them. Christ is the image of God and anything else misses the mark and comes up short of His glory. Once again, the Word is a mirror and mirrors don't lie. Let's look at what the mirror says about you:

- You are more than a conqueror

- Greater is He that is in you than he that is in the world
- You are chosen for greatness
- You were accepted in the beloved
- You are a new creation in Christ
- You are the head and not the tail
- You are His workmanship, created in Christ and unto good works
- You are a king and priest unto your God
- Royalty is flowing through your blood
- You are a citizen and an ambassador in the Kingdom of God
- You are part of the royal family
- You take part in a Kingdom that's bigger than this world
- You are part of a holy nation
- You are a son of the Living God

The enemy uses the world and all its images to pollute your imagination; he comes to steal, kill and destroy your imagination with vain imaginations.

> For the weapons of our warfare are not carnal, but mighty through God to the pulling down of strong holds; casting down imaginations, and every high thing that exalteth itself against the knowledge of God, and bringing into captivity every thought to the obedience of Christ. - 2 Corinthians 10:4,5

God has given us this incredible power of imagination. The mental images we imagine become seeds and we conceive those ideas in our mind. Your mind is the womb, and your mouth is your birth canal. Your imaginations, good or bad, become images and as those images increase into stronger impressions every day, they become your reality.

When God made mankind in His likeness and image, He created him out of His own imagination. You were a thought before you were a reality. God imagined you and He dreamed about you and now you're His dream come true. When God created my son Christian Mark, He must have had basketball on His mind. When the Lord created my wife, He must have had music on His mind, and when God created me, He must have had preaching on His mind. One day, all three of us tapped into the mind of God by His grace and began to walk in that which we were created to be. So many people have not tapped into the potential of God's imagination for them.

Verily I say unto you, Whosoever shall not receive the kingdom of God as a little child shall in no wise enter therein. - Luke 18:17

Children have incredible imaginations, but most parents just see it as a wild mind, and they squash their dreams. Jesus pointed to children many times in the Gospels and told us to become like them to enter the Kingdom. As a young child at five years old, I would imagine myself preaching to many people. With my little New Testament in hand, I would act it out by standing on the hearth of my grandma's fireplace on Sunday afternoons and preach to my family. Little did I know that one day what I imagined then would become a reality. I pray this book sanctifies your imagination through the Word of the Lord. Without a sanctified imagination, we cannot receive the Kingdom of God and all its benefits. There could be no true vision without exercising your imagination. A dream and vision fulfilled is an imagination or thought expressed openly. Jesus was the expressed image of the Father, or shall we say it this way: Jesus was the Father's highest image expressed in the earth. So are you and me to be in this world. I want my life to express the Father and fulfill His dream for my life. We are God's thoughts expressed in the world. The enemy wants to distort, corrupt, and destroy the image of God in you. From birth, demons desired to pollute God's image in you. But these are glorious days to be alive, for in these last days the Lord is fearfully and wonderfully fashioning His people in His likeness and image.

The enemy will use unclean images such as fear, worry, doubt, and anxiety. These produce thoughts like I'm not good enough, I can't do that, and I can't be that. Fears create images of negative things in our future, but we are to cast down false imaginations and that is our greatest warfare. By sanctifying our imaginations, we can truly live out of the reality of who we are in Christ. My wife had six miscarriages before she gave birth to our son, Christian Mark. In the six times she became pregnant prior to our son being born, she only made it to the first trimester each time. When she finally became pregnant with our son, she had many complications. I remember lying in bed every night and using my God-given imagination to envision me playing ball with my son. Night after night, I would see myself playing with my son until it became a reality. When my son was born, the umbilical cord was wrapped around his neck. As the enemy tried to destroy the images that I had of my son, those images God gave me were much stronger than the enemy's plan! I'll never forget the first time we played basketball and baseball together; at that moment, I was living out of the images that I created while my wife was carrying him in her womb. When the doctor gives you a negative report, do not allow that image to influence your thoughts, but go to the Word of the Lord and find the image of you being made whole because of the stripes Jesus endured. Remember the truth that He took your infirmities and bore your sicknesses at the whipping post. Make that the true image of your health.

> *For I know the thoughts that I think toward you, saith the Lord, thoughts of peace, and not of evil, to give you an expected end. Then shall ye call upon me, and ye shall go and pray unto me, and I will hearken unto you.*
> *- Jeremiah 29:11,12*

The Amplified translation reads, "to give you a hope and a final outcome." Your Heavenly Father has imagined your end and the outcome of your future will be peace and not evil, good and not bad! I want you to see your future, that the best is yet to come. God sees your end as greater than your present reality.

Simply stated, authentic prophecy is God's image of you.

> *According as he hath chosen us in him before the foundation of the world, that we should be holy and without blame before him in love - Ephesians 1:4*

Before you were ever in the belly of your mother God saw you and imagined you saved, sanctified, and filled with Heaven's Holy Ghost. He saw you powerfully advancing the Kingdom. While you were still lost and living in sin, He saw you complete and in Christ.

> *Then the word of the Lord came unto me, saying, Before I formed thee in the belly I knew thee; and before thou camest forth out of the womb I sanctified thee, and I ordained thee a prophet unto the nations. - Jeremiah 1:4,5*

God will call you before you become what He called you to be. Once He speaks it, He creates it. We cannot be who we are if we are being what everyone else wants us to be. We must live out of the true image of God for us. We can't be what God wants us to be if we conform to man's demands.

We must live by His definition of us and His definition alone. And if God put you in the belly of your mama, then He has need of you. There is no such thing as illegitimate children, only illegitimate parents. Whether you were conceived by your parents on their honeymoon night or in the backseat of a car, no one is a mistake.

> *Now the Lord is that Spirit: and where the Spirit of the Lord is, there is liberty. But we all, with open face beholding as in a glass the glory of the Lord, are changed into the same image from glory to glory, even as by the Spirit of the Lord. - 2 Corinthians 3:17,18*

As a man thinks in his heart, so is he. What you think about, you will bring about, what you behold is what you'll become, and what you see is what you will see. Prophetic imagery is so powerful that God will hasten His word to perform it when you see it and start saying it.

> *Then said the Lord unto me, Thou hast well seen: for I will hasten my word to perform it. - Jeremiah 1:12*

God's Word is His image of you. Therefore, prophesy His Word daily over your life.

> *Death and life are in the power of the tongue: and they that love it shall eat the fruit thereof. - Proverbs 18:21*

You have a birth certificate and a death certificate in your mouth. You have the power to bring life to some things and put other things to death. There are some things you have to assassinate. As David said, "We must put a watch before our mouth," being careful of the things we say. In the Kingdom of God, there are no surrogate sayers; you have to be the one to open your mouth and say something. Richard Williams told his two little girls, Venus and Serena, that one day they would win the U.S. Open and win the Wimbledon. Those words created that reality in those little girls' lives. Earl Woods put a golf club in the hands of his little boy named Tiger and said you will win the British Open, the U.S. Open, the PGA and the Masters and low and behold, Earl's words came to pass. Speak words of life over your children's futures and put the proper image of God in them. Parents have an incredible role to play in their children's lives. Through prophetic gifting, we should see our children's futures before they can see their tomorrow. It's called prophetic imagery. My wife and I lay hands on my son and declare over his life what God has called him to be and what we have declared over his life is coming to pass day by day, week by week, month by month and year by year.

> *Train up a child in the way he should go: and when he is old, he will not depart from it. - Proverbs 22:6*

> *And Caleb stilled the people before Moses, and said, Let us go up at once, and possess it; for we are well able to overcome it. - Numbers 13:30*

> *If the Lord delight in us, then he will bring us into this land, and give it us; a land which floweth with milk and*

honey. Only rebel not ye against the Lord, neither fear ye the people of the land; for they are bread for us: their defence is departed from them, and the Lord is with us: fear them not. - Numbers 14:8,9

Moses prophesied the Israelites would come into a land flowing with milk and honey. Two years later, 12 spies were sent to view the land; 10 came back with an evil report, but 2 of them came back with a prophetic report. You can't live a prophetic life with a pathetic mind. The word evil is a derivative of two words: wrong and thinking. Jesus taught us to pray "deliver us from evil" and all of us need to be delivered of wrong thinking. These 10 spies had the wrong thoughts, which kept them out of the Promised Land. But Joshua and Caleb thought right. Therefore, God said they had another spirit, and that spirit was the Holy Spirit. Ten came back with an evil report of huge giants in the land and said, "We look like grasshoppers in their sight." Their image of themselves was weak and not the image that God portrayed to them through Moses. Caleb and Joshua disagreed with the pathetic words given by the 10 negative spies. In Numbers 14, Caleb rose with a different image than the 10 spies and said, "These giants are bread for us." In Caleb's eyes, these giants were just bread. Think about bread for a minute: bread can't hurt you, bread can't bite you, and bread can't kill you. It's just bread, and that was Caleb's perspective of these giants. What if each and every one of us looked at the giant circumstances in our life and called them "just bread?" They declared their true image of what God said about them and 38 years later, Caleb and Joshua experienced the reality of their prophetic imagery by crossing over into the Promised Land that flowed with milk and honey. They decreed it and their decree became a reality.

Thou shalt also decree a thing, and it shall be established unto thee: and the light shall shine upon thy ways. - Job 22:28

IF GOD STARTED A WORK IN YOU, IT'S THE EVIDENCE THAT HE WILL COMPLETE IT.

When you look into the mirror of the Word of God, the man in the mirror is the real you. Learn to give the Holy Ghost a voice in your life and watch His image of you come to pass. Don't forget that the devil is a liar. You will fulfill your dream, you will walk in the promises of God, and you will become what God said you will become. Rise and live out of the unseen, projected prophecies that have gone over your life. Through prophetic imagery, speak over your day and over your future. If God started a work in you, it's the evidence that He will complete it. That's why Paul said,

"I'm confident of this very thing that He who has begun a good work in you will perform it!"

> *Declaring the end from the beginning, and from ancient times the things that are not yet done, saying, My counsel shall stand, and I will do all my pleasure. - Isaiah 46:10*

God declares the end from the beginning, He calls forth in the present what you will be in the future. Paul said, "He calls things that are not as though they were." The natural man calls things that are the way they are, but the spiritual man calls things that are not as though they were. The word declare in Hebrew means to 'bring forth.' When we make decrees, we are bringing forth that which is in the spirit realm into the natural realm. God declares the end before He even begins, and the end governs all the processes in your life. His purpose and will for your life will come to pass if you agree with the Word of the Lord like Joshua and Caleb did. He is Alpha and Omega, the beginning and the end. When He shows up as Alpha and begins something in your life, then you know in the process of time, Omega will show up and finish it. If you have seen Him as Alpha, then get ready to meet Omega. All God's promises are yes and amen; that prophetic dream that God has given you is just your destiny screaming at you!

> *Either what woman having ten pieces of silver, if she lose one piece, doth not light a candle, and sweep the house, and seek diligently till she find it? And when she hath found it, she calleth her friends and her neighbours*

together, saying, Rejoice with me; for I have found the piece which I had lost. Likewise, I say unto you, there is joy in the presence of the angels of God over one sinner that repenteth. - Luke 15:8-10

Luke 15 is a chapter of lost things that were restored: a lost sheep, a lost coin, and a lost son. When you look at a coin, it has an image on the front of it. The woman in this story represents the church who, in this hour, must seek diligently to restore the image of God back to the house of the Lord. It's time for the church to rise and diligently sweep the house until we recover our true image in Christ. It's time for the kings to arise!

CHAPTER 9

A King's Excellence

One purpose for writing this book is to help other people catalyze their destiny. This begins with understanding your identity as a king. Academic revelatory knowledge is not enough to reveal this kingship role; we need culture and climate to develop as kings. In the book of Numbers chapter 11, we see Moses put his kingly mantle on 70 men; 70 is the number for kingship and dominion. Moses was a kingmaker who raised up 70 kings who carried the same wisdom, anointing, and authority found in Moses. The anointing that was on Moses came upon them (Psalms 133).

After these things, the Lord appointed other seventy also, and sent them two and two before his face into every city and place, whither he himself would come. - Luke 10:1

In a similar manner, Jesus sent out men as Kingdom ambassadors. Again, we see the number 70 representing kingship and dominion, and He gave them power.

And the seventy returned with joy, saying, Lord, even the devils are subject unto us through thy name. - Luke 10:17

Jesus restored their true identity as kings so they could have dominion wherever He sent them. The results were incredible! The 70 men returned rejoicing over the mighty miracles that they performed in His name. But Jesus instructed them to not rejoice because of their dominion, but to rejoice because of their restored identity in His Kingdom as kings. Their birth certificate was in Heaven.

EVERYTHING THAT YOU WISH TO ACCOMPLISH FOR THE KINGDOM OF GOD FLOWS OUT OF YOUR IDENTITY AS A KING.

As a born-again, spirit-filled believer, you are in the bloodline of Jesus Christ. You changed families from the Adam's family to the family of Christ Jesus. For all of time, there have only been two men in the planet:

Adam and Christ. Either you are in one family or the other, so choose well. You're a son of God (males and females) in His Kingdom. God's Kingdom is the only Kingdom where every citizen is called to be a king. To qualify as a king, the only requirement is to be a son of a King. As the 70 kings returned to Jesus, they rejoiced over all the miracles. If we are going to recover the supernatural back in the church of Jesus Christ, we must first recover our kingship. Jesus was a priest and king; as a priest, He took charge of atmospheres and as a king He performed the miraculous. Everything that you wish to accomplish for the Kingdom of God flows out of your identity as a king. As a result of His kingship, Jesus performed miracles. When Pontius Pilate asked Him if He was a king, Jesus responded, "For this cause I have come." If He had not been a king, He could not have saved, healed, provided, delivered and performed all the signs and wonders that He did.

For as he thinketh in his heart, so is he: Eat and drink, saith he to thee; but his heart is not with thee. - Proverbs 23:7

When people ask you who you are, how do you respond? How do you successfully describe yourself?

1. Your thoughts create your words.
2. Your words create your attitude.
3. Your attitudes create your actions.
4. Your actions create your habits.

5. Your habits create your character.
6. Your character creates your destiny.

What words best describe you? Remember, this is not for others as much as it is for you to know. It's vitally important that you know who you are, what you have, and what you are called to do in this life. How do you respond when someone asks you what you do? It's very important that you have the proper image of yourself so you can flow in the measure of dominion needed to fulfill your destiny. Remember, the first person you lead in life is you! Once you have a clear image of who you are in Christ, then you must identify your gift cluster. Your gift cluster is what you were born with, while your acquired skills are what you do with your gifts. So, what are you good at? David's gift was his slingshot, but his acquired skill was what he could do with that slingshot like take out lions, bears, and giants.

Revelation gives you the right to pursue your purpose. I had a revelation as a young boy to preach, but I had a serious speech impediment. I did not let that hinder my pursuit of God and His call upon my life to preach the Word. At 12, God supernaturally healed my tongue when I was filled with the Holy Ghost. God healed my stuttering tongue for the glory of God. As a king in God's Kingdom, you will need to be well organized, structured, aligned, and in proper rank, or you will miss the opportunities that God has for you. I encourage you to do an assessment of your resources. Ask yourself what you have and what can you do. Your success will rise and fall on your ability to take an inventory of your resources, organize them, and then steward what you have. Please, if you find an excuse, don't pick it up. In every season, you will have one shot, one chance, one opportunity to make a difference. David had one chance to take out Goliath. Esther had one chance to expose Haman. Gideon had one chance to deliver Israel. Joseph had one chance to feed the people in time of famine. Jehu had one chance to take out Jezebel. Your objective should be for God to give you one chance. God does not move in an event, but through a people. By creating the proper culture and climate, we invite Heaven by sending it a signal that we are ready for God to use us. Honor, stewardship, excellence, servanthood, and preparation create the culture and climate to facilitate a move of God in our lives. These key components will attract Heaven and gain you personal favor. It's necessary to discover the gift you are and the gifts you have. First, discover who you are, then determine what you have. From there, you can develop what you have, to later display what you have. Everything you have need of is already encrypted in your spirit for your next season. There's more to you than what meets the eye!

> *Every good gift and every perfect gift is from above, and cometh down from the Father of lights, with whom is no variableness, neither shadow of turning. - James 1:17*

I've learned to not only celebrate the gifts that people have, but more importantly, the gift that they are. Every one of you that is reading this book is a perfect gift sent from Heaven into the earth to influence and transform your world as a king and priest.

I cannot conclude this chapter without talking about the power of excellence. We must fight for excellence because it honors God and inspires people.

> *And the king communed with them; and among them all was found none like Daniel, Hananiah, Mishael, and Azariah: therefore stood they before the king. And in all matters of wisdom and understanding, that the king enquired of them, he found them ten times better than all the magicians and astrologers that were in all his realm. - Daniel 1:19,20*

Everyone who is in Christ's Kingdom should aspire to be a 10. God has a standard in which He measures our level of excellency. It was clear the Hebrew boys were considered 10s in the eyes of God. If there are 10s in the Kingdom of God, then there must be ones, twos, threes, fours, etc. If you are a five, you need to work better to become a 10 in the eyes of Heaven. If you are a leader and you are a five in God's Kingdom, you can only raise people up to be a one, two, three, four or five. You will never take people beyond the level that you are. Every one of us is born a one; no one is born a ten. In like manner, excellence is not a gift, and no one is born with it. It's an attitude that is catalyzed by a right spirit. The future belongs to those who have the edge of excellence. Churches, businesses, ministries, and networks all rise and fall on the spirit of excellence. Excellence is maximizing the gifts that God has given you. What you have been given and what you do with what you have must be developed to the highest degree. Never function below your innate abilities.

PEOPLE OF EXCELLENCE ALWAYS MAKE IMPROVEMENTS AND NEVER MAKE EXCUSES.

Excellence will overcome what normal people complain about. Most people complain about never succeeding in life because they're so busy complaining about why they can't find any success and how they never will. Pursue excellence and you will always rise to the top of your sphere.

And whosoever shall compel thee to go a mile, go with him twain. - Matthew 5:41

Jesus made the statement if someone compels you to go a mile, then go two miles. He is explaining that excellence always goes the extra mile. I cringe when people say the phrase, "That's good enough." But good enough is not great. You don't have to ask someone if they walk in the spirit of excellence. You can easily tell by how they dress, manage their time, by their conversation, their attitude, their behavior, their worship, etc. People of excellence always make improvements and never make excuses. Those with this spirit stand out in the crowd. People of excellence never settle for average, but they always press beyond into surpassing greatness. God did not save you to be an average person; He saved you and filled you with His Holy Spirit to be a person of excellence.

Everyone must make excellence a way of life.

Be kindly affectioned one to another with brotherly love; in honour preferring one another. - Romans 12:10

Excellence manifests itself by honoring and preferring other people better than yourself. Jesus was a giver, not a taker. There are only two men in the world: Adam and Christ. You are either in Adam or you're in Christ. Adam lived as a taker and Christ lived as a giver. Please choose well. People of excellence give more than they take in life.

But the Lord was with Joseph, and shewed him mercy, and gave him favour in the sight of the keeper of the prison. And the keeper of the prison committed to Joseph's hand all the prisoners that were in the prison; and whatsoever they did there, he was the doer of it. The keeper of the prison looked not to any thing that was under his hand; because the Lord was with him, and that which he did, the Lord made it to prosper. - Genesis 39:21-23

Joseph had a spirit of excellence that promoted him everywhere he landed: at Potiphar's house, in the prison house, and finally, in the courts of Pharaoh. Even amid contradicting circumstances, he maintained a spirit of excellence. Joseph had many obstacles to overcome before he fulfilled his destiny. But through every test that he faced, his spirit of excellence remained intact. Excellent people are over-comers, while average people are copper-outers. Excellence takes ownership of whatever you do in life. At 16, I was hired to work at a flower shop in my city. On my first day, my father drove me to the shop. As I was getting out of the car, he grabbed my hand and asked me where I was going. I told him I was going to work. He said, "No, you're not, don't go in there unless you can give this company 110%." My father instructed me to treat the flower shop like it was my own, as though someday it could be mine. He told me to mop the floors like they belonged to me and to scrub the toilets as if I owned them. So I followed his instructions and worked with the spirit of excellence, and within a few years, the owner of a competing floral shop noticed me, offering me a job with him. I accepted the offer and went to work for the new company, following my father's wisdom, and in the same way, treating the new company as if it was my own. Little did I know that by the time I was 27 years old, I would be partners in one of the top florists in America, and within a short time, I would be the sole owner of this very flower shop. The spirit of excellence would not let me off the hook. It promoted me to the top of my field, allowing me to fulfill the dream of owning my business. Since then, we've expanded our company to another location and have risen to the top 500 florists out of 30,000 in the world. It was an insatiable need for excellence that allowed us to accomplish this success. If you can't do it right, don't do it until you're ready. Prepare by giving yourself to the spirit of excellence and watch God bless and promote you for His glory.

> *For as he thinketh in his heart, so is he: Eat and drink, saith he to thee; but his heart is not with thee. - Proverbs 23:7*

If you think excellent, you will be excellent. Excellence is a decision, not a gift.

> *And the Lord shall make thee the head, and not the tail; and thou shalt be above only, and thou shalt not be beneath; if that thou hearken unto the commandments of the Lord thy God, which I command thee this day, to observe and to do them. - Deuteronomy 28:13*

Quit comparing yourself with average people. You were not born to be average; you were born to be excellent. You were designed to be the head and not the tail, above and not beneath. It is the spirit of excellence that will make you the head above all others.

> *Let the righteous smite me; it shall be a kindness: and let him reprove me; it shall be an excellent oil, which shall*

not break my head: for yet my prayer also shall be in their calamities. - Psalms 141:5

This powerful passage of Scripture reveals that excellence is an oil — it's an anointing. We can receive this oil of excellence when we're under the right kingmaker leadership.

O Lord our Lord, how excellent is thy name in all the earth! - Psalms 8:9

And whatsoever ye do in word or deed, do all in the name of the Lord Jesus, giving thanks to God and the Father by him. - Colossians 3:17

The Psalmist said the Lord's Name is excellent. Paul stated that whatever you do in word and deed, do it in His Name. His Name is excellent; therefore, to do it in His Name is to do it with excellence. Everything we do in life should be done in the spirit of excellence. Excellence is that which is superior and above the rest. When you are above the rest, you bring glory to your Heavenly Father. We must be excellent in all aspects of life: in our attendance, in our honor, in our worship, in our giving, in our service, in our work ethics, in our vernacular, in our relationships, and even how we manage our time.

Herein is our love made perfect, that we may have boldness in the day of judgment: because as he is, so are we in this world. - 1 John 4:17

God is a God of excellence and as His representatives in the world, we should represent the spirit of excellence on His behalf.

Excellence is a spirit that is never satisfied. Excellence is doing common things in an uncommon way. Excellence is a prevailing spirit that will defeat every one of your enemies and empower you into the top of your field of influence. Excellence inspires people like nothing else. We all must fight for the spirit of excellence because it honors God and everyone in our world. The spirit of excellence means trouble for the powers of darkness. Hell shutters at the thought of you being a person of excellence.

EXCELLENCE INSPIRES PEOPLE LIKE NOTHING ELSE.

Excellence has been hijacked in the church. It's time that we recover it and take it back.

> *Ye said also, Behold, what a weariness is it! And ye have snuffed at it, saith the Lord of hosts; and ye brought that which was torn, and the lame, and the sick; thus ye brought an offering: should I accept this of your hand? Saith the Lord. - Malachi 1:13*

In the book of Malachi, God rebuked the children of Israel

for bringing Him sacrifices that were sick and lame. He told them either to bring Him the best lamb or bring Him nothing at all. In everything we do, we must offer the best. It's clear in this passage that God does not receive average, weak sacrifices. He requires the best! What if we gave Him the best offerings, our best service, our best worship, our best gifts, and our best attitude? It is within our ability to give Him the absolute best, with the spirit of excellence, and as a result, the Lord will honor our best by giving us His best.

> *And when the queen of Sheba had seen all Solomon's wisdom, and the house that he had built, And the meat of his table, and the sitting of his servants, and the attendance of his ministers, and their apparel, and his cupbearers, and his ascent by which he went up unto the house of the Lord; there was no more spirit in her. - 1 Kings 10:4-5*

This is an amazing story of the excellent spirit that King Solomon carried. When the Queen of Sheba came to visit him, the excellence she saw took her breath away. The excellence that King Solomon used to build the house of the Lord attracted God, gold, and the glory. When the world comes to visit our churches (like the Queen of Sheba visited Solomon's temple), instead of visiting foolishness and ignorance, the world should come and see excellence, wisdom and glory. As kings in Christ's Kingdom, we have been chosen to be a people of excellence that display the glory of God in everything we do.

CHAPTER 10

True Worshipers

In chapter 4 of the Gospel, according to John, is a beautiful story of a true worshiper. While passing through Samaria, Jesus came to Jacob's well. At the same time, a Samaritan woman was coming to draw water from that well.

> *Here cometh a woman of Samaria to draw water: Jesus saith unto her, Give me to drink. - John 4:7*

This Samaritan woman was surprised that Jesus, a Jew, would ask her for a drink, as Jews had no dealings with Samaritans. Samaria was a city that the Jews would avoid because it was a refuge for outlaws. Both groups had a great hate for one another, creating segregation among the races.

In the eastern culture, it was improper for men to speak to a woman unless asking for a drink. Jesus answered and said unto her,

> *If thou knewest the gift of God, and who it is that saith to thee, Give me to drink; thou wouldest have asked of him, and he would have given thee living water. - John 4:10*

This woman was about to get a revelation of the gift of God that was sitting on the well in front of her.

Jacob's well represents anything that man draws from outside of Jesus, from any external source. When a man is not drawing from the life of Christ, he will turn to things that satisfy his flesh that take his attention away from Jesus. Hell wants to channel your thirst to anywhere else except Jesus. Avoid things that quench your thirst for Jesus; learn to acquire a taste for the things of God. This woman asked Jesus if He was greater than their father, Jacob. This present generation is about to find out how great our God really is. He's about to display His greatness in and through His emerging kings for all the world to see.

> *O taste and see that the Lord is good: blessed is the man that trusteth in him.- Psalms 34:8*

I love this passage, for it is a key for you and me to see the goodness of God manifested in our lives. Tasting comes before seeing. As we develop a thirst for the Lord and the things of God, the results will be that we will see and experience the goodness of God right here in the land of the living.

When this woman arrived at Jacob's well, she saw The Well sitting on a well!

Therefore with joy shall ye draw water out of the wells of salvation. And in that day shall ye say, Praise the Lord, call upon his name, declare his doings among the people, make mention that his name is exalted. Sing unto the Lord; for he hath done excellent things: this is known in all the earth. Cry out and shout, thou inhabitant of Zion: for great is the Holy One of Israel in the midst of thee. - Isaiah 12:3-6

She was about to draw from the wells of salvation and forever be changed.

Jesus saith unto her, Go, call thy husband, and come hither. The woman answered and said; I have no husband. Jesus said unto her, Thou hast well said; I have no husband: For thou hast had five husbands; and he whom thou now hast is not thy husband: in that saidst thou truly. The woman saith unto him, Sir; I perceive that thou art a prophet. - John 4:16-19

This woman tried to fill the void with other relationships outside of Jesus, just like so many today. I gave my life to Jesus when I was nine years old and was filled with the Holy Ghost, March 7, 1971, at 11. I ran from the call of God upon my life at 14 and did not return to the Lord until I was 28 years old. During that time, I tried to fill my life and satisfy the void with everything else but Jesus, while knowing all the time nothing would satisfy me like Him. Once I returned to Christ, He alone satisfied my thirst! This woman went from husband to husband, just like so many Christians today when they go from church to church, from conference to conference, from house to house, job to job and even relationship to relationship to fill the emptiness. But only Jesus can fill that void. We are to go from glory to glory, from faith to faith, and from strength to strength, and that can only come from an intimate relationship with Jesus Christ.

He asked this woman to give him a drink. God has no needs, He only has desires and if we satisfy His desires, He will meet all of our needs. We don't talk very often in church about God's desires, but the focus is always on our desires and needs. Most people come to Jesus to get a drink and get their needs met. They talk about their thirst and their hunger. But what about the Lord's thirst and His desires? They know Him only as their merciful high priest who can meet their needs, but they have never met Him as their King, who demands their obedience and desires their worship and intimacy.

This whole story is really a revelation of true worshipers. Every Sunday morning around the world, multitudes come to a worship service to worship the Lord and we think that satisfies Him. He's not seeking worship; He is seeking worshipers. Worship is more than a Sunday morning event; it is a lifestyle. True worship really begins Monday and carries on through Saturday. We worship the Lord by how we raise our children and we worship in the way we work. We worship in our giving of tithes and offerings. We worship the Lord by honoring one another–this is true worship.

> *Jesus saith unto her, Woman, believe me, the hour cometh, when ye shall neither in this mountain, nor yet at Jerusalem, worship the Father. Ye worship ye know not what: we know what we worship: for salvation is of the Jews. But the hour cometh, and now is, when the true worshippers shall worship the Father in spirit and in truth: for the Father seeketh such to worship him. God is a Spirit: and they that worship him must worship him in spirit and in truth. - John 4:21-24*

Jesus has one desire: He is thirsty for our praise, worship, service, obedience, fellowship, and intimacy.

I grew up being told that Jesus came and died on the cross so I can go to Heaven. That is not the original purpose and intent for which Jesus came and died on the cross. At the cross, He spoke these two words that say it all, "I thirst!" He wasn't thirsty for a drink of water, not at all. It was His thirst for intimacy with you and me that drove Him to the cross. Because of Adam's transgression, we were all separated from God by our sins. So, God, by the death of His Son, reconciled us so His life could save us and enter into fellowship with Jesus Christ. Now that His blood justified us, we can have an intimate relationship with Him. While Jesus was suspended on the cross between Heaven and earth, He declared, "I thirst," and today, He is still thirsty for an intimate relationship with each one of us. If you are thirsty for intimacy with Christ, then you are numbered among the true worshipers in this hour who will also give Jesus a drink.

After Jesus ministered to this woman, she threw away her water pot and became a water pot that led an entire city to Jesus. It's impossible to taste the goodness of God and not share it with others. True evangelism will always result from drinking from the Spirit of Christ. Only as we drink from these living waters in times of intimacy, can we pour out living waters to mankind. There must always be up-reach to Him before there is outreach to others. Before Jesus visited the city, He visited this woman, then He visited the city through the woman. In the days in which we live, the Lord intends on visiting our cities through the church of Jesus Christ. He will not bypass the church. The church is still His vehicle for city transformation.

In John chapter 2, we see Mary, Jesus, and the disciples at a wedding feast in Cana. They had run out of wine at the celebration and desired more wine.

And when they wanted wine, the mother of Jesus saith unto him, They have no wine. - John 2:3

Every time the church transitions from one season to the next, the Lord will let the old wine run out before He pours out the new wine. Maybe some of you are experiencing a season when you are running out. Maybe you're running out of patience, running out of strength, running out of joy, running out of friends, but please don't run out on God! It's only a sign when the old runs out that the new is about to come. Be patient. The time will come when the old runs out and He will pour out the new into your life. He always saves the best wine for last; the best is yet to come! When they were thirsty for more, the season shifted. Stay thirsty!

Thirst is the currency of heaven.

Ho, every one that thirsteth, come ye to the waters, and he that hath no money; come ye, buy, and eat; yea, come, buy wine and milk without money and without price. - Isaiah 55:1

Years ago, while looking at this verse, I thought it strange and didn't understand the key to buying the new wine. The Lord says anybody who is thirsty can come, even those who do not have money. They can come and buy wine and milk without money and without price. I thought, how can you buy wine and milk without money? Then the Holy Spirit shed light on this passage by directing me to go back and read the first words of the verse, "Everyone that is thirsty!"

And there it was. I saw it for the first time that we can buy the new wine with our thirst for Jesus. Just like we use dollars here in America to exchange for the provision that we need in life, likewise, thirst is the currency of Heaven. In God's economy, thirst is the point of exchange.

Jesus had not performed a miracle prior to this wedding feast, but it was their thirst that became the catalyst for the miraculous. Because of their thirst, Jesus turned water into wine and this was "the beginning of miracles."

This beginning of miracles did Jesus in Cana of Galilee, and manifested forth his glory; and his disciples believed on him. -John 2:11

The key to walking in the miraculous is thirst, thirst alone will release miracles in and through your life. Once again, tasting comes before seeing! Our thirst for Jesus results in experiencing the miraculous. Everywhere I travel, the body of Christ is crying out for miracles, and I remind them when they finally get thirsty enough, the miracles will begin. People desire to see the miraculous, but they're not thirsty enough for Jesus.

In the last day, that great day of the feast, Jesus stood and cried, saying, If any man thirst, let him come unto me, and drink. He that believeth on me, as the scripture hath said, out of his belly shall flow rivers of living water. (But this spake he of the Spirit, which they that

believe on him should receive: for the Holy Ghost was not yet given; because that Jesus was not yet glorified.)
- John 7:37-39

Jesus shared this revelation to His disciples during the celebration of The Feast of Tabernacles. It's important we understand at which feast He was sharing this revelation. There are three major feasts that Israel celebrated annually: The Feast of Passover, The Feast of Pentecost, and The Feast of Tabernacles. These three feasts are types and shadows of the realities that we experience as God's new creation. When you asked Jesus into your life, and were born again by the Spirit of God, that was your Passover. If you have received the baptism of the Holy Ghost and are filled with the Spirit of God, that was your Pentecost. For the last 2,000 years, the church has been celebrating Passover and Pentecost, but there is another feast on the horizon known as The Feast of Tabernacles. Many Bible scholars teach this feast will not happen until we go to Heaven. That teaching is not scriptural. The first two feasts of Passover and Pentecost blessed you, but The Feast of Tabernacles (which is the next feast on God's agenda) is not just a blessing to you, but God's blessing through you to others. In this next feast, there will be living waters that are flowing out of you, touching all creation. We see here in this passage that Jesus says you must drink first and then waters will flow out. This is a divine order in God. We must draw from the Spirit of God in an intimate relationship so we can pour our living waters on creation to bring healing, deliverance, and salvation everywhere we go. Metaphorically, the Holy Spirit is a river, and this river dwells in you. The Holy Spirit is a river, not a lake, not a pond or a puddle. He is a moving thing that cannot be hindered. He is an unstoppable, unquenchable, and unapologetic force that cannot be limited. This powerful river is resident within you and me.

I can tell who has been drinking from the Spirit of God because they are springing up and flowing out with living waters. If you were drawing from the Spirit of God, you can expect everything to spring up in your life, such as joy, peace, revelation, health, love, and creativity. There will be side effects and an overflow of the Christ that is within you. We cannot control the direction of the river, but we can influence it by our thirst. It is the Spirit of God that will flow wherever He chooses. I love this: Jesus did not say that one river would flow out of you, but rivers (plural) would flow out of your belly.

There are three rivers that are inside every spirit-filled believer right now:

- **River of Worship:** The priest inside of you is a worshiper, one who releases mercy and compassion.

- **River of Witness:** The prophet inside of you is a witness, one who declares God to man.

- **River of Warfare:** The king inside of you is a warrior, one who rules and reigns in authority.

A witness is one who provides evidence. The reason we have people in our world running to psychics is because we have very few witnesses in Christ's Kingdom. But a new priesthood is on the rise with kings, priests, and prophets emerging today to be a witness of the resurrection power of Jesus Christ in all the earth. I call these three rivers the Kingdom rivers—a kingly river, a priestly river, and a prophetic river flowing through you and me. Greater is He that is in you than he that is in the world. You are chosen for greatness! Your thirst for God releases the greatness that is resident within. From before the foundation of the world, you were chosen as one of God's VIPs–a "very important person." You are one of a kind, exceptional in every way, and fearfully and wonderfully made. You are delightfully diverse with assorted giftings, anointings, and divine energies. You have something to do that no one else can do or say in the planet. God has a

YOU ARE DELIGHTFULLY DIVERSE WITH ASSORTED GIFTINGS, ANOINTINGS, AND DIVINE ENERGIES.

glorious divine plan that includes you. If the Greater One lives in you, and He does, how can you not do great things?

Blessed are they which do hunger and thirst after righteousness: for they shall be filled. - Matthew 5:6

Once again, drinking from the Spirit of God comes first, then a flow of miracles and healing will follow. Every miracle results from intimacy with King Jesus. In these days, God is not wanting to come down to us but He wants to come out of us. Christ is in you, the hope of glory, and in the words of Job, "My help comes from within." You can't give away what you don't have, and you can only get what you need to give away from the Spirit of Christ, Who is our source. Jesus told His disciples at the wedding feast to draw out now. It's time to draw out now!

And three of the thirty chiefs went down, and came to David in the harvest time unto the cave of Adullam: and the troop of the Philistines pitched in the valley of Rephaim. And David was then in a hold, and the garrison of the Philistines was then in Bethlehem. And David longed, and said, Oh, that one would give me a drink of the water of the well of Bethlehem, which is by the gate! And the three mighty men brake through the host of the Philistines, and drew water out of the well of Bethlehem, that was by the gate, and took it, and brought it to David: nevertheless he would not drink thereof, but poured it out unto the Lord. - 2 Samuel 23:13-16

This wonderful story of David and his mighty men takes place by the wells of Bethlehem. The armies of the Philistines surrounded them. At one moment, King David longed to have a drink of water from the wells of Bethlehem. Bethlehem means the house of bread; it is a type of the church of Jesus Christ, and we, being many, are one bread. Listen to the still, small voice of our Heavenly David who whispers that He longs to have a drink from the wells of Bethlehem. Jesus wants a drink from the well that you and I are. The word Philistine means to roll in ashes or dust, thus representing our flesh. Don't let your flesh keep you from giving your heavenly David a drink. The word longed in the Hebrew means to desire, to crave, and to covet. Can you hear the whisper from the throne of God as He craves to have a drink from His church? Three of David's mighty men broke through the Philistine army to get a drink of water for David and brought it back to him to quench his thirst. Refusing to drink the water, David poured it back out in the earth. When we give King Jesus a drink to satisfy His thirst, He takes what we've given Him, opens the Heavens, and pours it back out into our earth.

These three mighty men represent your breakthrough in three areas of your life: spirit, soul, and body. If you need a breakthrough, give Him a drink by satisfying His thirst and watch the Lord pour out a blessing that there will not be room enough to receive. Satisfying His desire will be a catalyst for our own personal breakthrough. The well was by the gate in Bethlehem. Isaiah said that His gates shall be called praise; your praise and worship satisfy the desire of Christ's thirst for intimacy with you. May each one of us arise with a passion to draw from the well of salvation that Jesus is, but also to satisfy and quench His thirst by ministering to Him. May we all be sensitive to the whisper coming from Heaven that says, "I THIRST," calling us to a deeper, intimate relationship with Jesus.

CHAPTER 11

The Sons of God

I have glorified thee on the earth: I have finished the work which thou gavest me to do. - John 17:4

When Jesus therefore had received the vinegar, he said, It is finished: and he bowed his head, and gave up the ghost. - John 19:30

At the cross, Christ Jesus finished His mission on earth through His death, burial, and resurrection. This was the first appearing of Jesus upon the earth, but at the end of this age, He will appear again through His sons (male and female) and do greater works through them.

Verily, verily, I say unto you, He that believeth on me, the works that I do shall he do also; and greater works than these shall he do; because I go unto my Father. - John 14:12

Here's the question, what are the greater works that Jesus was referencing in this passage of Scripture? Many people think it's performing more miracles than Jesus ever did in His earthly ministry. That may be true, but I think there's more to the Scriptures that unveil what Jesus really meant by greater works as in Isaiah chapter 61.

> *The Spirit of the Lord God is upon me; because the Lord hath anointed me to preach good tidings unto the meek; he hath sent me to bind up the brokenhearted, to proclaim liberty to the captives, and the opening of the prison to them that are bound; To proclaim the acceptable year of the Lord, and the day of vengeance of our God; to comfort all that mourn; To appoint unto them that mourn in Zion, to give unto them beauty for ashes, the oil of joy for mourning, the garment of praise for the spirit of heaviness; that they might be called trees of righteousness, the planting of the Lord, that he might be glorified. And they shall build the old wastes, they shall raise up the former desolations, and they shall repair the waste cities, the desolations of many generations. And strangers shall stand and feed your flocks, and the sons of the alien shall be your plowmen and your vinedressers. But ye shall be named the Priests of the Lord: men shall call you the Ministers of our God: ye shall eat the riches of the Gentiles, and in their glory shall ye boast yourselves. For your shame ye shall have double; and for confusion they shall rejoice in their portion: therefore in their land they shall possess*

the double: everlasting joy shall be unto them. - Isaiah 61:1-7

Jesus fulfilled the first two verses of Isaiah's prophecy.

And he came to Nazareth, where he had been brought up: and, as his custom was, he went into the synagogue on the sabbath day, and stood up for to read. And there was delivered unto him the book of the prophet Esaias. And when he had opened the book, he found the place where it was written, The Spirit of the Lord is upon me, because he hath anointed me to preach the gospel to the poor; he hath sent me to heal the brokenhearted, to preach deliverance to the captives, and recovering of sight to the blind, to set at liberty them that are bruised, to preach the acceptable year of the Lord. And he closed the book, and he gave it again to the minister, and sat down. And the eyes of all them that were in the synagogue were fastened on him. And he began to say unto them, This day is this scripture fulfilled in your ears. - Luke 4:16-21

After Jesus had been tested and proven faithful for 40 days in the wilderness, He went to His hometown. On the Sabbath day, He opened the book of Isaiah to chapter 61. After reading the first two verses, He closed the book, gave it to the minister, and sat down. This is a prophetic picture of what Jesus did after He ascended into Heaven when He sat down at the right hand of His Father, turning the rest of His work over to His ministers, the body of Christ. The Spirit of the Lord was upon Jesus and anointed Him to deliver the blind, the bound, the beggar, the broken and the bruised. Jesus fulfilled His part of Isaiah's prophecy, but verses 3 through 7 have yet to be fulfilled. That assignment will be fulfilled by Jesus' end-time, glorious church. The same Spirit on Jesus is the same Spirit that is upon us to also minister to the blind, the bound, the beggar, the broken and the bruised. But we will do the greater works as well by fulfilling verses three through seven. He promised He would give us glory for our sufferings, the oil of joy for our mourning, and a mantle of praise for the spirit of heaviness. We will display His splendor, rebuild ancient ruins, renew ruined cities, and restore the places that have been devastated for generations. The prophecy names us the priests of the Lord and ministers of our God. Just as Jesus turned the book over to the minister and sat down in Luke 4, He did likewise when He ascended in Acts chapter 1. Turning His ministry over to His ministers, the church, He then went and sat down at the right hand of the Father in heavenly places. This prophecy also explains how the promises of greater works include the wealth of the nations flowing into the church. For all our shame, disappointment, and delays, He will give us a double portion.

THE SAME SPIRIT ON JESUS IS THE SAME SPIRIT THAT IS UPON US

These are exciting days to be alive in the planet. Yes, these are the days of greater works, when God is going to give us a double portion of His Spirit, meaning that we will fulfill the second portion of the promises in Isaiah 61. The first appearing of Jesus upon the earth was glorious as He finished the work the Father sent Him to do, but at the end of this age, He will appear again through His sons to do greater works. The finished work of Calvary is the foundation that guarantees that His second work through the sons of God will be successful.

> *And there were certain Greeks among them that came up to worship at the feast: The same came therefore to Philip, which was of Bethsaida of Galilee, and desired him, saying, Sir, we would see Jesus. Philip cometh and telleth Andrew and again Andrew and Philip tell Jesus. And Jesus answered them, saying, The hour is come, that the Son of man should be glorified. Verily, verily, I say unto you, Except a corn of wheat fall into the ground and die, it abideth alone: but if it die, it bringeth forth much fruit. He that loveth his life shall lose it; and he that hateth his life in this world shall keep it unto life eternal. If any man serve me, let him follow me; and where I am, there shall also my servant be: if any man serve me, him will my Father honour. Now is my soul troubled; and what shall I say? Father, save me from this hour: but for this cause came I unto this hour. Father, glorify thy name. Then came there a voice from heaven, saying, I have both glorified it, and will glorify it again. - John 12:20-28*

In verse 28 Jesus asked His Father to glorify His name, and

the Father responded from Heaven saying, "I have both glorified it and I will glorify it again." The first glorification was through the only begotten Son, Jesus Christ, but He will be glorified again in His body at the end of this age. The Apostle Paul promised us that there would be a glorious church without spot or wrinkle. May I say it this way—there will be a church of glory: a people filled with the glory of God and carriers of His glory into all the earth. The sons of God will manifest the glory of God in all the earth fulfilling Numbers 14:21.

In the Old Testament, the law prophesied these two comings of Christ in the type and shadow of Elijah and Elisha. Elijah represents the type of Jesus Christ, while Elisha is the type of the end-time body of Christ. When Elijah was taken up, Elisha received a double portion of anointing of Elijah's spirit.

> *And Elijah took his mantle, and wrapped it together, and smote the waters, and they were divided hither and thither, so that they two went over on dry ground. And it came to pass, when they were gone over, that Elijah said unto Elisha, Ask what I shall do for thee, before I be taken away from thee. And Elisha said, I pray thee, let a double portion of thy spirit be upon me. And he said, Thou hast asked a hard thing: nevertheless, if thou see me when I am taken from thee, it shall be so unto thee; but if not, it shall not be so. And it came to pass, as they still went on, and talked, that, behold, there appeared a chariot of fire, and horses of fire, and parted them*

both asunder; and Elijah went up by a whirlwind into heaven. And Elisha saw it, and he cried, My father, my father, the chariot of Israel, and the horsemen thereof. And he saw him no more, and he took hold of his own clothes, and rent them in two pieces. He took up also the mantle of Elijah that fell from him, and went back, and stood by the bank of Jordan; And he took the mantle of Elijah that fell from him, and smote the waters, and said, Where is the Lord God of Elijah? And when he also had smitten the waters, they parted hither and thither and Elisha went over. - 2 Kings 2:8-14.

Elisha received his request for a double portion of anointing and did twice the miracles that Elijah performed. So shall it be at the end of this age with the sons of God. We will walk in the double portion anointing. When Elijah was taken up, his mantle fell down. You never take your anointing to Heaven with you when you leave the planet. There is no need for your anointing there. The anointing destroys yolks, and there are no yolks in Heaven. Heaven is doing okay; it's the earth that needs your anointing where the bondages exist in the nasty now and now. Let's look at this pattern. Jesus ascended into Heaven in Acts chapter 1, but His mantle came down on 120 believers in the upper room in Acts 2. When Jesus died, His overall work was not yet finished. It takes two comings of Christ, each with a distinct mission, to fulfill the Word of God in Isaiah 61. Elisha was completely sold out in his pursuit of his spiritual father Elijah. Compare his journey with the 50 prophets at Bethel and 50 prophets at Jericho. These other prophets had the revelation and present-day truth that Elijah was going to be taken up, but they refused to walk with Elisha as he pursued Elijah. There are many people that know what God is about to do in the earth and can articulate it to others, but not everyone is willing to follow Jesus all the way to the Jordan. The Jordan is the place of surrender, death to self, and sacrifice. Distance is dangerous. You can know what the Lord is doing, but not enter it. It's not good enough to have present day truth. You must apply it and walk it out in shoe leather. What was the criteria for Elisha receiving the double portion anointing? Elijah said, "If you see me when I ascend, then you'll receive the double portion." We must keep our eyes on our heavenly Elijah, Jesus Christ, at all times. Do not focus on the supernatural or the blessings, but fix our eyes on Him. We are to follow Christ and the miracles will follow us. Elijah did not say, "When you see the chariots of fire or the whirlwind coming...." No, he said, when you see me ascending, you'll receive the double portion. We are to look solely at Jesus, who is the Author and Finisher of our faith. If our focus is on King Jesus, then the supernatural, signs, and wonders will follow us. I want you to see the type and shadow in Elijah's ascension and how it relates to what God is about to do in and through the church of Jesus Christ in this hour. The church of Jesus Christ has seen Jesus in His death. Look at our friends, the Catholics, who have made this their priority, and still keep Him on the cross with their crucifixes. This represents that they see Him in His death, paying the price for the forgiveness of our sins. But there's so much more in God. Our good friends, the Baptists, have seen Him in His burial. If you belong to a Baptist church, they will baptize you in water in faith to bury the old man and your past life before the new birth. Our Pentecostal brothers and sisters have seen Jesus in His resurrection walking as a new creation in the newness of life. But like Elisha, we must see Jesus in this present hour in all aspects of His death, burial, resurrection, and ascension! There is a generation at the end of this age that will see Him in His ascension, seated at the right hand of the Father, with all His enemies underneath His feet. His body, the church, will walk in the authority and power that Jesus received and walked in. All power was given to Him after the resurrection, but after His ascension, He gave it to His disciples. He did not take it with Him to Heaven; He gave it to us. Yes, all principalities, powers and spiritual wickedness remain subject to Jesus. Since they are under His feet, they are also under our feet, His body. Elijah is a type of Jesus who finished his work and passed into the Heavens, leaving his mantle behind. Likewise, we must rise up as a company of Elishas and pick up the mantle of our heavenly Elijah, Jesus Christ, to finish the work we've been sent to do. Elisha is a type of the end-time, prophetic church who will follow Jesus all the way into their double portion inheritance. Elisha picked up Elijah's mantle, which he smote the Jordan, a picture of death. At the cross, Jesus smote sin, sickness, poverty, and death once and for all. Like Elisha, let's pick up Jesus' mantle, and by faith, violently smite the Jordan as a second witness. Appropriate the finished work of Jesus Christ by faith. I want Jesus' life repeated in mine! And that's my prayer for you, that Jesus' life would be repeated in yours like Elijah's life was repeated in Elisha's. There is a generation of Kingdom sons who will walk in double for all their trouble. They keep their eyes on Jesus! Jesus went up; His mantle stayed down. Let's pick up Jesus' mantle as a second witness and subdue every enemy. The call on this generation is to bring all our enemies under our feet. Let us arise and go to our Jordan, the lowest place, the place of death itself, in submission to the Lord and the place of humility. If we humble ourselves under the mighty hand of God, He will raise us up in due season.

Elijah had an unstoppable anointing because he was locked into finishing. Whatever has come to stop you, to get you to throw in the towel and become idle, shake yourself and rise to take your seat of authority!

> *Shake thyself from the dust; arise, and sit down, O Jerusalem: loose thyself from the bands of thy neck, O captive daughter of Zion. - Isaiah 52:2*

You are anointed to finish! There is a spirit in you right now called the Holy Spirit, who is driving you to a place called finish. We need a finishing mindset; we are the generation called to finish what Jesus started. We must be locked into finishing this work, putting our hands to the plow, and not looking back. No other generation has been called to finish. Other generations have been called to start and others were glory carriers of their progress, but we are the generation called to finish what they began. What their hands have started, our hands will finish. This is why our forefathers cannot help us in this next season. I'm so thankful they brought us to this day and gave us a firm foundation, but in the words of Joshua: we have never come this way before. We will not use a map that reveals where someone has already been, but we must use the compass of the Holy Spirit to enter new dimensions of the Kingdom of God. Circumstances, people's opinions, and adversity can't move you; you must revolve your life around Kingdom cause. It's bigger than you and me, it's about a generation waiting for the sons of God to take their rightful place and deliver creation. Nothing can deter you and me from finishing. We are crafting the end together. If you stay on course, God will send you the resources and capable people to finish your destiny. We must now pick up our mantle and finish the work.

And that, knowing the time, that now it is high time to awake out of sleep: for now is our salvation nearer than when we believed. - Romans 13:11

But if he will not hear thee, then take with thee one or two more, that in the mouth of two or three witnesses, every word may be established. - Matthew 18:16

Jesus needs a second witness to finish the work, and the sons of God are called to be that witness to finish what Jesus left for us to do. Get ready. Part two of God's glorious plan is on the horizon, and a new day is dawning.

> *Behold, I will do a new thing; now it shall spring forth; shall ye not know it? I will even make a way in the wilderness, and rivers in the desert. - Isaiah 43:19*

The work will not be finished until all creation is restored through the rule and reign of Christ Jesus on the earth, in and through the sons of God. The sons of God must mature in this season and as they do, they will manifest the nature and the ministry of the Lord Jesus Christ in all the earth.

> *For the earnest expectation of the creature waiteth for the manifestation of the sons of God. - Romans 8:19 KJV*
>
> *For all creation is waiting eagerly for that future day when God will reveal who his children really are. - Romans 8:19 NLT*

These sons of God will be the first fruits of God's creation. Assigned to bless all the families of the earth, they fulfill the promise given to Abraham's seed.

> *And I will bless them that bless thee, and curse him that curseth thee: and in thee shall all families of the earth be blessed. - Genesis 12:3*

I tell our church family that we may not be able to bless the families of the entire world, but we can bless the families of our territory. During the COVID-19 pandemic, our church has given close to $10 million in food to our community. We've given tens of thousands of dollars away in household goods, automobile supplies, healthcare and beauty supplies, and clothing. We are custodians of a food distribution called the NOW Project, (Nourishing Others' Well-being) where thousands of people come in lines of vehicles to receive multiple boxes of food to sustain them through the pandemic. Our intercessors and pastors go to the vehicles to minister and pray for those in need. This is just one way that we've been able to bless the families of our community and fulfill the promise given to Abraham and his seed, that all the families of the earth will be blessed.

Regardless of what religious people may think or say, this is God's designed plan to set creation free from its bondage to sin, sickness, and corruption and usher it into the freedom and the glory of the children of God.

And I will bless them that bless thee, and curse him that curseth thee: and in thee shall all families of the earth be blessed. - Romans 8:21

Until this glorious plan is complete, there is still work yet to be finished. God has given us the Church Age to prepare for the Age of the Kingdom. Our process and preparation is never wasted in Christ. There is no true loss in Christ. There is only gain, gain through loss, life through death, glory through shame, power through weakness, and exaltation through abasement. In this present season, the Holy Spirit, through His five-fold leaders (apostles, prophets, evangelists, pastors, and teachers), is training and equipping the sons of God for this exciting mission. We are in training for reigning. The sons of God must put on the mind of Christ, grow up in Christ's Kingdom culture and exercise their authority as kings in the earth, even as Christ exercised His authority as a king when He walked the earth, for He is the pattern Son.

Create in me a clean heart, O God; and renew a right spirit within me. - Psalms 51:10

Perfection is not required, but the right spirit is. None of us are perfect, which is why Jesus paid the price and shed His blood at Calvary. The blood of Christ is as powerful today as it was 2,000 years ago. It never loses its power. It is still warm and still wet, redeeming man from his sinful ways. If we are a people that are in hot pursuit of God, who are presence driven, living in a spirit of repentance and forgiveness, walking in love, truth, humility, and servanthood, then God will use us during this next move of the Spirit. King David was a forerunner of this end-time priesthood of kings that rule and reign with Christ upon the earth over all their enemies.

According as he hath chosen us in him before the foundation of the world, that we should be holy and without blame before him in love. - Ephesians 1:4

Chosen in Christ before the foundation of the world, we

were foreordained and placed in His Kingdom for such a time as this!

For many are called, but few are chosen. - Matthew 22:14

These shall make war with the Lamb, and the Lamb shall overcome them: for he is Lord of lords, and King of kings: and they that are with him are called, and chosen, and faithful. - Revelation 17:14

We are heirs of God and joint heirs with Christ.

And if children, then heirs; heirs of God, and joint-heirs with Christ; if so, be that we suffer with him, that we may be also glorified together. - Romans 8:17

Jesus is the firstborn among many brethren, and your elder Brother. We are kings and priests, part of His royal family of sons.

For it became him, for whom are all things, and by whom are all things, in bringing many sons unto glory, to make the captain of their salvation perfect through sufferings. - Hebrews 2:10

So powerful is this royal family of Kingdom sons that creation is on tiptoe waiting for them to appear. We are called to pray for the sick and they will recover, raise the dead, open blind eyes, and cast out devils.

And these signs shall follow them that believe; In my name shall they cast out devils; they shall speak with new tongues; They shall take up serpents; and if they drink any deadly thing, it shall not hurt them; they shall lay hands on the sick, and they shall recover. - Mark 16:17-18

If you believe the words you speak, then creation will respond to your words. Sickness and disease must obey.

Therefore, I say unto you, What things soever ye desire, when ye pray, believe that ye receive them, and ye shall have them. - Mark 11:24

When you speak over your family, your family aligns with Heaven. As priests, we pray and as kings we say. He gave us authority that whatever we loose on earth shall be loosed in Heaven and whatever we bind on earth shall be bound in Heaven.

And I will give unto thee the keys of the kingdom of heaven: and whatsoever thou shalt bind on earth shall be bound in heaven: and whatsoever thou shalt loose on earth shall be loosed in heaven. - Matthew 16:19.

We are called to speak in the earth whatever is true in Heaven and whatever is not true in Heaven; we are to bind it in the earth. We have been given the keys, the authority, and the permission to lock and unlock, to permit and not permit. There is no Coronavirus in Heaven, therefore it's not permitted here in your earth. As kings in God's Kingdom, we are to release the realities of Heaven here on planet earth.

Thy kingdom come, Thy will be done in earth, as it is in heaven. - Matthew 6:10

The Kingdom of God is a realm of words and power where our words of life swallow up death.

All creation is designed to respond to a son of God. Adam's disobedience caused catastrophes. Creation fell into the bondage of corruption, but creation only responds to a son. When Adam violated his sonship, the earth responded with thorns and thistles. When Cain quit acting like a son, the Heavens closed over him. When the prodigal left his position and function as a son, he fell into famine. When a son rebels against God, creation responds. When the prodigal son joined the wrong people, he ended up eating leftovers. Today, when the sons of God connect with wrong networks, organizations, and people, they forfeit genuine revelation settling for yesterday's manna. When Israel, God's son, was abused in Egypt, creation become violent and spewed out 10 plagues upon the Egyptians. When the sons of God complained, the waters become bitter at Marah and snakes attacked and bit the children of Israel. When Noah, the son of God, obeyed by building God an ark, creation responded. The Heavens opened, flooding the world with water in righteousness judgement. When the sons of Korah disobeyed God in rebellion, an earthquake opened the ground and consumed them. When Lot fled Sodom and Gomorrah, there was no son left in the city and judgment fell. When cities have no corporate son, there will be failing economies, climate changes, environmental catastrophes, and demonic infiltration in that city. Religious organizations, illegitimate systems, seeker friendly ministries, and para churches will fill the void of sonship in cities. Creation is groaning for the manifestation of the sons of God. Through the sons of God, the Son of God, Jesus Christ, will be manifested in His nature and ministry in all the earth. On the cross, the Son of God was abused, and creation responded. The sun turned dark, and the earth quaked in sorrow for His death. In cities with no sons, we see pestilence, sickness, famine, lack, poverty, wickedness, and perversions of all kinds. But where there are sons, we see an opened Heaven, deliverance, salvation, prosperity, health, and the blessing of the Lord resting upon that city.

The blessing of the Lord, it maketh rich, and he addeth no sorrow with it. - Proverbs 10:22

It's time for the sons of God to arise.

Arise, shine; for thy light is come, and the glory of the Lord is risen upon thee. For, behold, the darkness shall cover the earth, and gross darkness the people: but the Lord shall arise upon thee, and his glory shall be seen upon thee. - Isaiah 60:1,2

Our local church, Jubilee Ministries, here in New Castle, Pennsylvania, has been designed to be a reception hall for the Kingdom of God. Here is where we usher our congregants into the Kingdom of God, releasing their potential and revealing their true identity in Christ as the sons of God. When you were born into the Kingdom you were born into greatness.

Ye are of God, little children, and have overcome them: because greater is he that is in you, than he that is in the world. - 1 John 4:4

How could you not be chosen and do great things if the Greater One is resident within you right now? You are not common people anymore; you're royal heirs of King Jesus. Your new birth was a miracle. Miracles should be normal for you. You were raised from death to life. As royalty flows through your veins, so should the miraculous. There is a present stirring in my spirit to destroy your appetite for casual Christianity and prepare you for a life of the miraculous. It's my prayer that the words of this book will shift you into a new level of thinking.

Let this mind be in you, which was also in Christ Jesus. - Philippians 2:5

Most Christians are presently content with what I would call a pre-Kingdom mentality. There are many Christians today who are born again and spirit filled, but have a John the Baptist mentality. John the Baptist proclaimed the Kingdom, yet never manifested it. He declared the Kingdom of God but could not demonstrate its power.

And labour, working with our own hands: being reviled,

we bless; being persecuted, we suffer it. - 1 Corinthians 4:20

John's first words were, "Repent, for the Kingdom of God is at hand." While he could proclaim the Gospel of the Kingdom, he could not demonstrate it because he lacked the power. We never see him casting out devils or healing the sick. He never raised the dead or opened deaf ears and blind eyes. John the Baptist spoke against evil that was in his present world, but had no power to eradicate it. Most John the Baptist Christians today lack power; they have much rhetoric but have no reality of the Kingdom of God operating in their lives. John the Baptist believed in miracles, declared the authority of the Kingdom, but did not walk in it. John the Baptist came in the spirit of Elijah but lacked the power of Elijah.

And Jesus answered and said unto them, Elias truly shall first come, and restore all things. - Matthew 17:11

Jesus came in the spirit and the power of Elijah. He declared on the Mount of Transfiguration that Elijah was still going to come and restore all things. This is not Elijah of the Old Testament; this is a prophetic picture of an Elijah company that will come at the end of the age and restore all things in the earth. He declared this would take place in the future: a company of men and women who would not only come in the spirit of Elijah but in the power of Elijah. Our purpose and intent in this chapter is to shift you from just declaring the Kingdom to manifesting it. The Kingdom of God does not come in word alone, but in power.

Verily I say unto you, Among them that are born of women there hath not risen a greater than John the Baptist: notwithstanding he that is least in the kingdom of heaven is greater than he. - Matthew 11:11

Jesus made this tremendous accolade concerning John the Baptist stating that no one born of women was greater than John. No one prior to Jesus Christ, who was born of women, was greater than him. But John was born of a woman's womb, not out of the womb of the Spirit. Herein lies the key to Kingdom authority and power. The least who are born again in Christ's Kingdom are considered greater than John the Baptist.

And from the days of John the Baptist until now the kingdom of heaven suffereth violence, and the violent take it by force. - Matthew 11:12

The Bible says that from John until the present moment when Jesus was speaking, the Kingdom of God suffered violence and only the violent could take it by force. John violently struggled to enter the Kingdom but couldn't because he was not born in the Kingdom.

Jesus answered and said unto him, Verily, verily, I say unto thee, Except a man be born again, he cannot see the kingdom of God. Nicodemus saith unto him, How can a man be born when he is old? can he enter the second time into his mother's womb, and be born? Jesus answered, Verily, verily, I say unto thee, Except a man

> be born of water and of the Spirit, he cannot enter into the kingdom of God. That which is born of the flesh is flesh; and that which is born of the Spirit is spirit. Marvel not that I said unto thee, Ye must be born again.
> - John 3:3-7

You must be born again to see, enter, and show the Kingdom of Heaven on earth. Jesus, the pattern Son, was born in the Kingdom, and everyone born of the Spirit of Christ is born into the Kingdom of God as sons. Religion has hijacked the true identity of sons of God from the church. Once again, my purpose in this chapter is to shift you from a pre-Kingdom mentality into the Kingdom of sons.

> Herein is our love made perfect, that we may have boldness in the day of judgment: because as he is, so are we in this world. - 1 John 4:17

The Word tells us that as He is, so are we in this world, present tense, right now. It's not in the future; Jesus is a Son and so are you. Yes, dearly beloved, we are like the pattern Son, Jesus Christ, right now. We are victorious as He is victorious, holy as He is holy, righteous sons as He is a righteous Son.

> For he hath made him to be sin for us, who knew no sin; that we might be made the righteousness of God in him.
> - 2 Corinthians 5:21

This is your present reality. The reason the Kingdom of God has suffered is that religion has stolen your true identity and position in Christ as a son.

> *Beloved, now are we the sons of God, and it doth not yet appear what we shall be: but we know that, when he shall appear, we shall be like him; for we shall see him as he is. -1 John 3:2*

John was only a friend of God, but he was not a son of God since you must be born again to get that position. The Lord called many people His friend prior to the new covenant including Abraham, Moses, and John the Baptist. As glorious as that may be, we are more than just a friend of God. We are sons of the Living God, who are part of His royal family right now. My son, Christian Mark (he was 18 years old when I wrote this book) is not my friend. He is my son, and that's the highest relationship that anyone could have with me. The revelation of sonship releases the keys of authority and power into your life. As a son of God, you have the right to give some things power or take its power away; everything runs by power in the universe. Your cars run by power, your microwaves run by power, your cell phones, and even demons run by power, and so does the Kingdom of Heaven. God will always back the righteous decisions of a son. I said all this to tell you the supernatural power of God flows and operates out of your identity in Christ as sons. As a son of God, you have a commission to bring the supernatural realities of Heaven upon the earth.

A new race is emerging in the earth known as the sons of God. The Spirit of the Son that is resident within you right now has the power to transform everything around you by its intrinsic nature. In God's Kingdom, goodness swallows up evil and light swallows up darkness.

> *Ye are all the children of light, and the children of the day: we are not of the night, nor of darkness. - 1 Thessalonians 5:5*

> *Ye are the light of the world. A city that is set on a hill cannot be hid. Neither do men light a candle, and put it under a bushel, but on a candlestick; and it giveth light unto all that are in the house. Let your light so shine before men, that they may see your good works, and glorify your Father which is in heaven. - Matthew 5:14-16*

God has not given us a spirit of fear, but of love, power, and a sound mind; every son is equipped with these three blessings. The sons of God do not fear darkness because they know greater is He that is in them than that which is in the world. They know that the environment does not control them, but they control the environment. The sons of God speak the Word into darkness. We should believe what we believe and if we do, we speak out what we believe. Good is more powerful than evil, for we overcome evil with good.

> *Be not overcome of evil, but overcome evil with good. - Romans 12:21*

The highest title in God's Kingdom is not an apostle,

prophet, evangelist, doctor or a millionaire. The highest name given to man is son. This title is eternal, while apostle, prophet, and evangelist are temporary. In the Kingdom you are not Irish, Italian, German, or of African descent because all our roots trace back to Adam or Christ. There are only two men in the planet: Adam and Christ. Choose well between Adam, the taker, and Christ, the giver. You must choose every day whether you will live out of the Adamic nature or live out of Christ's nature, the new creation man. Inside this Scotch-Irish body of mine, I am a son of God. I am a citizen of another Kingdom. I'm a new creation in Christ, and a king in Christ's Kingdom. In Adam, all men die, but in Christ, all men will live.

> *Ye are of God, little children, and have overcome them: because greater is he that is in you, than he that is in the world. - 1 John 4:4*

You and I have come out of God. Don't identify with this world. It's all a matter of your position. As long as you identify with Adam, you identify with sickness, sorrow, death, fear, lack, depression, sin, and darkness. But when you identify with Christ, you are identified with His Kingdom, life, joy, peace, righteousness, faith, wholeness, love, and health.

> *Who hath delivered us from the power of darkness, and hath translated us into the kingdom of his dear Son. - Colossians 1:13*

As a young boy growing up in the church, I remember

how people identified more with what they came out of than what they were coming into. Most testimonies I heard detailed how God delivered them from sin and brought them out of the bars and their addictions. Those are wonderful testimonies, but there is so much more in God ahead of us. Didn't Paul say, "Your eye has not seen your ear has not heard, nor has it entered in your heart the things that God has prepared for you?" Your future is really bright. Yes, He has delivered us out of darkness, but He has also translated us into the Kingdom of His dear Son. We should be majoring on what God is bringing us into and not the life He brought us out of. Let's identify with the new life and not the old life.

If I believe that greater is He that is in me, then I am not subject to anything outside of me. There are no limitations, restrictions, contradictions, threats, or oppositions that can stop a son of God. The family of God in Heaven and on earth has been named sons. There is no higher name, not even angels have this name. Only sons can deliver creation.

For God so loved the world, that he gave his only begotten Son, that whosoever believeth in him should not perish, but have everlasting life. - John 3:16

Any time God wants to bring change, He sends a son. You are a son that has been sent to reign in this present life and to bring change. Reign means to change things.

For if by one man's offence death reigned by one; much

more they which receive abundance of grace and of the gift of righteousness shall reign in life by one, Jesus Christ. - Romans 5:17

The world's greatest problem is that they have not seen a son; they've seen religion, they heard our doctrines; they watched our marriages fail, and they have seen the Western church's greed for wealth. But in this next season, they are getting ready to see the sons of God who are assigned to set creation free, for only sons can be free and set creation free.

If the Son therefore shall make you free, ye shall be free indeed. - John 8:36

Since we were seated with God in Christ in heavenly places, the right hand is the position of a son. It is the posture of power, dominion, favor, and inheritance. In my house, as sons, we carry the presence of the Lord; no demon in hell can get in. Possessing the Father makes us sons. It was a Spirit of the Father on Jesus that made Him a Son.

The Spirit of the Lord is upon me, because he has anointed me. - Luke 4:18a

With the Spirit of the Lord upon Him and as a Son, Jesus corrected everything that was out of order. He brought days of Heaven upon the earth. There is no sickness in heaven, therefore, He made sure there was no sickness in His world. He healed everyone that came to Him with physical maladies. As sons, everything in earth should not invade us, our homes, or our cities. We, however, should invade the earth with Heaven. We are the sons of God called to realign the earth to look just like Heaven.

That your days may be multiplied, and the days of your children, in the land which the Lord sware unto your fathers to give them, as the days of heaven upon the earth. - Deuteronomy 11:21

Chapter 12

The Foot Company

My purposeful intent in this book is to show the reader an end-time revelation of the church's true identity and calling in this new season, where the Lord is leading us. In this chapter, we will unveil the Foot Company and expand on the characteristics of this many-membered unit.

> *How beautiful upon the mountains are the feet of him that bringeth good tidings, that publisheth peace; that bringeth good tidings of good, that publisheth salvation; that saith unto Zion, Thy God reigneth! – Isaiah 52:7*

Everything concerning God's new creation man is in the Word of God concealed in an encrypted form.

It is the glory of God to conceal a thing: but the honour of kings is to search out a matter. - Proverbs 25:2

As kings in God's Kingdom, we have been given the privilege to search out the deep things in God; they are not hidden from us, but they are hidden for us. God speaks in dark sayings, and by the Spirit of God, we unravel them to decode them. These mysteries hide in a language that the natural mind does not understand.

> *And the disciples came, and said unto him, Why speakest thou unto them in parables? He answered and said unto them, Because it is given unto you to know the mysteries of the kingdom of heaven, but to them it is not given. For whosoever hath, to him shall be given, and he shall have more abundance: but whosoever hath not, from him shall be taken away even that he hath. Therefore speak I to them in parables: because they seeing, see not; and hearing they hear not, neither do they understand. - Matthew 13:10-13*

In this passage of Scripture we see Jesus distinguishes the disciples from other people by using "you" and "them." God speaks in allegories; the Bible was not written for mere men, but it was penned for the sons of God.

> *Wherefore I will not be negligent to put you always in remembrance of these things, though ye know them, and be established in the present truth. - 2 Peter 1:12*

It is not good enough just to know God's present day truths and mysteries in the glorious days of our time; they must be applied. Established means to abide; they must abide in our hearts. Truth must be contained in the inward parts of our hearts. The phrase "abide in you" means that it must become a living reality in your life, and when it does, the Scripture can be fulfilled. When Jesus said if you abide in Him and His words abide in you, then you shall ask whatever you will and it will be done (literally created) for you. When the Word becomes flesh in your life, then you can rise as a king, speak creative words to the world where you live, and whatever you say shall come to pass. Religion has grand theories and philosophies, but religious people don't practice them.

TRUTH MUST BE CONTAINED IN THE INWARD PARTS OF OUR HEARTS.

> *How beautiful upon the mountains are the feet of him that bringeth good tidings, that publisheth peace; that bringeth good tidings of good, that publisheth salvation; that saith unto Zion, Thy God reigneth! - Isaiah 52:7*

> *And how shall they preach, except they be sent? as it is written, How beautiful are the feet of them that preach the gospel of peace, and bring glad tidings of good things! - Romans 10:15*

Paul quotes this passage of Scripture to the Roman church in a much more expanded revelation than Isaiah did. Paul did not misquote the Scriptures but by the Spirit, expanded what Isaiah prophesied. The Him who would bring good news is Jesus. Him, singular and masculine, represents Jesus Christ, who is the head. But in the new covenant, Paul makes the verse corporate to represent the body of Christ and prophesies that a "them" would bring good news. Jesus came and then multiplied Himself into them who would bring good news. Them is what we call the feet of Christ's body or the Foot Company. The feet are the part of the body in contact with the earth right now. Jesus is the designated head of the body; His church, the feet of Christ, will be known as the Foot Company. The entire family of God is in Heaven and earth, but this prophetic verse is for the part of the body of Christ presently in contact with the earth, which includes you and me.

> *And I heard him speaking unto me out of the house; and the man stood by me. And he said unto me, Son of man, the place of my throne, and the place of the soles of my feet, where I will dwell in the midst of the children of Israel for ever, and my holy name, shall the house of Israel no more defile, neither they, nor their kings, by their whoredom, nor by the carcases of their kings in their high places. - Ezekiel 43:6-7*

In another passage, the Lord said the Heavens are His throne, but something shifts in this passage when the throne moves from Heaven into the earth where His Foot Company is. He is saying that He will live among His Foot Company. Hallelujah! This is a place of His presence, where

His throne and His authority will dwell, where His feet are. We are the generation of the Foot Company that will be known as the people of His presence.

The glory of Lebanon shall come unto thee, the fir tree, the pine tree, and the box together, to beautify the place of my sanctuary; and I will make the place of my feet glorious. - Isaiah 60:13

I love how this passage says, "I will make the place of My feet glorious." These trees speak of the body of Christ, who are trees of righteousness, His Foot Company. This assembly will be recognized by its multi-ethnic interfusion. They are people without prejudice, with no racial, gender, or age-based bias among them. They will be given a ministry of reconciliation. We know Heaven is glorious, but we are promised that all the glories and riches of the Kingdom of Heaven will be manifested in and through the Foot Company here on planet earth.

When a baby is born, the head comes first, then the hands, and finally, the feet. Let's look at what I believe symbolizes the timing relative to birthing this new creation man in the earth in these end times.

Birthing the Body of Christ in End Times

- **Head–1950s and 1960s:** In these decades, we had

encounters with the face of God, including the latter rain movement, the great healing tent revivals, and the charismatic movement.

- **Hands–1970s, 1980s, and 1990s:** In these years, we encountered the hand of God, five-fold ministry of apostles, prophets, evangelists, pastors, and teachers. We learned how His hand provided through faith in the faith and prosperity message.

- **Feet–2,000s:** In the 21st-century, we will encounter the feet of God with the birthing of the Foot Company, hidden in the womb of preparation until this hour. It's time to birth the Foot Company!

God always saves the best for last! Jesus also stated that "the last will be first and the first will be last." Although the Foot Company has come last, they will be the first to walk in the Father's abundance and receive the inheritance of the saints in Christ Jesus.

The Psalmist in chapter 91 takes us from the natural realm of things into the spiritual realm. Verses 11-12 tell us He will give His angels charge over us to keep and protect us. They shall bear us up in their hands, so our feet are not smashed against a stone. This Foot Company will be given supernatural protection. Emerging out of the womb of preparation, they will not be victims of terrorism, accidents, disease, plagues, poverty, lack, fear, cancer, diabetes, or any other plague. Angels are dispatched to protect the Foot Company; they will be given spiritual immunity like no other generation. They will dwell in the secret place of God. The secret place is a culture in God of righteousness, peace, and joy in the Holy Ghost. It's a lifestyle of intimacy with Christ in His Kingdom. When you abide in this culture, then you have the promise of spiritual immunity.

And Jesus answered him, saying, It is written, That man shall not live by bread alone, but by every word of God. And the devil, taking him up into a high mountain, shewed unto him all the kingdoms of the world in a moment of time. And the devil said unto him, All this power will I give thee, and the glory of them: for that is delivered unto me; and to whomsoever I will I give it. If thou therefore wilt worship me, all shall be thine. And Jesus answered and said unto him, Get thee behind me, Satan: for it is written, Thou shalt worship the Lord thy God, and him only shalt thou serve. And he brought him to Jerusalem, and set him on a pinnacle of the temple, and said unto him, If thou be the Son of God, cast thyself down from hence: For it is written, He shall give his angels charge over thee, to keep thee. - Luke 4:4-10

And all they in the synagogue, when they heard these things, were filled with wrath, And rose up, and thrust him out of the city, and led him unto the brow of the hill whereon their city was built, that they might cast him down headlong. But he passing through the midst of them went his way. - Luke 4:28-30

This promise was given to the head, our Lord Jesus Christ, and the Foot Company, the end time church. It was already fulfilled in Jesus' life during His 3 ½ year ministry. Angels don't protect the saints in Heaven; they are dispatched to protect the saints on earth. It doesn't mean you escape trouble in the secret place; you just overcome trouble with angelic support.

This Foot Company is a company of kings who decree things that are established upon the earth.

> *Where the word of a king is, there is power: and who may say unto him, What doest thou? - Ecclesiastes 8:4*

It's important that you learn to make declarations as a saint, for they are vitally important.

> *Thou shalt make thy prayer unto him, and he shall hear thee, and thou shalt pay thy vows. Thou shalt also decree a thing, and it shall be established unto thee: and the light shall shine upon thy ways. - Job 22:27,28*

A decree that is established becomes a law, a rule, an order. It is a law made by a superior to govern inferiors. The superior Christ that lives in you has authority over all inferiors that are in your world. Did not John say, "Greater is He that is in you than he that is in the world?" Therefore, the atmosphere does not control the spirit, but the Spirit of Christ in you controls the atmosphere. Get used to making decrees over your family, your marriage, your children, your body, and your mind. Make decrees over your church family, your city, your nation, and the world. Start declaring 1,000 will fall by my side and 10,000 at my right hand, but it will not come nigh me. Put up some prophetic signs in the spirit telling the powers of darkness: no trespassing here, no hunting here, and no dumping here in my home. Create boundaries by telling your enemies they're not welcome here. Hell has absolutely no place in your life unless you give permission.

> *Be sober, be vigilant; because your adversary the devil, as a roaring lion, walketh about, seeking whom he may devour. - 1 Peter 5:8*

You must make it clear to the powers of darkness that they may not have your children, your marriage, your money, your ministry, your business, or your health. They cannot hunt and harass your children. Remember that you're packing power in the Holy Ghost, and every day that you wake up, the powers of darkness declare, "Oh no, they're still alive and well on planet earth!" Long enough, the powers of darkness have dumped their wicked ideologies and beliefs

THE ATMOSPHERE DOES NOT CONTROL THE SPIRIT, BUT THE SPIRIT OF CHRIST IN YOU CONTROLS THE ATMOSPHERE.

into our school systems. It's time that we raise up a new breed of teachers to reverse what hell has purposed to do in our children. The church must rise and say, "Enough is enough!" It's time to occupy our planet for King Jesus and make Him King over everything. When this Foot Company emerges, our houses and churches will come under spiritual immunity as God's promise to us. Get violent with your prayers, praise, and proclamations. We are promised that all our enemies will be placed under the Foot Company. This is powerful!

> *And ye shall tread down the wicked; for they shall be ashes under the soles of your feet in the day that I shall do this, saith the Lord of hosts. - Malachi 4:3*

> *The Lord said unto my Lord, Sit thou at my right hand, until I make thine enemies thy footstool. - Psalms 110:1.*

Nothing can stand against this anointed Foot Company—not cancer, diabetes, fear, or hatred. No demon in hell, no terrorist or drug demon, not even the spirit of death, will have power over them. Hell hates the thought of this company emerging in the earth today; it was bad enough to have one Son of God, now there's an entire company of sons increasing in the earth today.

> *And the God of peace shall bruise Satan under your feet shortly. The grace of our Lord Jesus Christ be with you. Amen. - Romans 16:20*

When you ask Christ into your life you have peace with

God, but as you grow in God, you become part of this company that exceeds just having peace; you now can make peace. Jesus made peace on the cross through His precious blood for you and me; it cost Him everything. God made peace through the blood of Jesus Christ. Peace does not just happen; we must make peace. Peace is an authority. Becoming a peacemaker will cost you and me everything as well. Peace is not tranquility, but relational harmony among the Foot Company. In ancient times, when a broken bone was fractured and then healed, they would say that the bone has come to peace. Why? It became stronger than it ever was. Once a bone has been fractured and healed, it is almost impossible to break that bone in the same place again.

Blessed are the peacemakers: for they shall be called the children of God. - Matthew 5:9

One of the greatest characteristics of the sons of God is their role as peacemakers. In the Greek, sons can be defined as father likeness; you can never be more like your Heavenly Father than when you are making peace! You have power to crush your enemies because of your peace. Paul never said the God of war will crush the enemy under your feet, but the God of peace will crush him under your feet. The Foot Company will crush every enemy under their feet in the coming days. The Apostle Paul said it was their obedience that was reported to them, and by their obedience, all hell will be wiped out. It's by an obedient people that hell will be wiped out. He did not emphasize this would occur by their faith, revelation, or even prayers, but by their obedience. Paul's prophecy was future tense; he used the word shall. As a second witness, the Foot Company will rise as peacemakers and bring all their enemies under their feet. Once again, you cannot be more like your Heavenly Father than when you're making peace.

There is a mighty, devil-crushing church emerging in the earth today.

And I will put enmity between thee and the woman, and between thy seed and her seed; it shall bruise thy head, and thou shalt bruise his heel. - Genesis 3:15

This verse gives us God's first promise made to man and the devil. It reveals that the seed of the woman would bruise the serpent and the serpent would bruise His heel. The heel is the most difficult part of the body to bruise. Why? Because it's calloused and tough. Jesus, the seed/offspring of the woman, bruised the head of the serpent at Calvary, and hell bruised His heel. At the end of this age, the Foot Company will enforce both the finished work of Calvary and this promise in the earth. Even the least in the Kingdom will have complete dominion over darkness, including little children, for of such is the Kingdom of Heaven.

The wolf also shall dwell with the lamb, and the leopard shall lie down with the kid; and the calf and the young lion and the fatling together; and a little child shall lead them. And the cow and the bear shall feed; their young ones shall lie down together: and the lion shall eat straw like the ox. And the sucking child shall play on the hole of the asp, and the weaned child shall put his hand on the cockatrice' den. They shall not hurt nor destroy in all my holy mountain: for the earth shall be full of the knowledge of the Lord, as the waters cover the sea. - Isaiah 11:6-9

Why is the Foot Company a faceless people? You will see their feet and not their faces. Those who want their faces to be seen possess a personality disorder. Either a spirit of pride or insecurity has impaired their personality because they have a need to be seen and receive attention. It's a desire for self-importance. But when you see the Foot Company you see the head, Christ Jesus, and not feet; you see Christ in the body. The feet are the most uncomely part of the body. If you are married, you did not marry your spouse because of their feet. As the most uncomely part of the body of Christ, this Foot Company will emerge as the most powerful part of His body to defeat all their enemies, bringing them under their feet.

But now are they many members, yet but one body. And the eye cannot say unto the hand, I have no need of thee: nor again the head to the feet; I have no need of you. Nay, much more those members of the body, which seem to be more feeble, are necessary: And those members of the body, which we think to be less honourable, upon these we bestow more abundant honour; and our uncomely parts have more abundant comeliness. - 1 Corinthians 12:20-23

This passage deals with relationships in the body of Christ and its members. The hand and foot are inseparable, they need one another. The feet of Christ need the hand (fivefold ministry) to fulfill their divine destiny in God. For it's the hand of God (apostles, prophets, evangelists, pastors, and teachers) that equips and the trains the Foot Company and empowers them to advance the Kingdom of God in their world.

He maketh my feet like hinds' feet, and setteth me upon my high places. - Psalms 18:33

King David prayed God would make his feet as a deer and thrust him into high places. This defines the Foot Company's ability to accelerate and ascend. Ascending to the top of their mountain, they will rule and reign with Christ.

To illustrate this point, let's look at biblical examples of acceleration:
- How about Elijah, how he outran his enemies? Oh, this is a glorious revelation! He told Ahab to get in his chariot to go to Jezreel because it was about to rain, but Elijah outran him by foot. Dearly beloved,

get ready to outrun all your enemies as the spirit of acceleration is coming upon the Foot Company.

- Remember in Exodus when Aaron's rod budded overnight? Now that's acceleration!
- In this season, the plowman overtakes the reaper; as soon as you get your seed in the ground, you will reap a harvest.
- The former rain and the latter rain fall at the same time to be poured out on one generation!
- Water turns into wine without the fermenting process.
- The woman who lived bent over for years suddenly stands straight in the synagogue, completely healed!
- A nation is born in one day!
- Elisha declared that this time tomorrow, the famine will be broken and there will be more than enough food in Samaria.

These demonstrate the power of acceleration; everything will move faster and faster in the coming days because it's a season of acceleration.

In the Gospel of John chapter 13, we see Jesus take off His garments, pick up a servant's towel, and wash the feet of His disciples. This is such a powerful, prophetic picture of the Foot Company, so let's unpack it. Garments represent rank and authority. Jesus was prophetically saying that He was laying down His authority to be a servant. Did He not teach that the greatest in the Kingdom would be the servant of all? He picked up a towel, a symbol of the lowest ranking individual in the culture of that day. The Foot Company will lay aside their social status, pride, ranking, and titles to pick up the towel and tub ministry. So many people say they have the Holy Ghost, but do not want to serve. It's utterly impossible to be filled with the Holy Ghost and not desire to be a servant. One of the names of the Holy Ghost is Helper; therefore, if you have the Holy Ghost, you will be a helper. When Jesus ascended to Heaven, He never stopped being a servant. In fact, He still serves via the Holy Ghost in and through the body of Christ today. Every time that you serve, it's Jesus serving through you. Let me encourage you if you belong to a local church, support your leaders with your time, your talents, and your treasure. Rise and serve the vision of the local church where you are a member. I think it's wonderful that we can watch services online; the technology of this day allows us to reach more people with the Gospel. But there's nothing like fellowshiping, serving, and worshiping the Lord together as the body of Christ. Jesus washed His disciples' feet preceding His ascension. Here lies the key to ascending into new places. You serve your way into authority; you serve your way into ministry, and you serve your way into success. Look at the example of Joseph. He served in Potiphar's house, then in the prison, and this led him to serving as Prime Minister in Pharaoh's court, where he ruled and reigned in the time of famine. The hand ministry in this hour is called to wash the feet of the Foot Company. I pray that this book and the writings within will wash the feet of the reader to walk in all that God has called you to walk in. As the Foot Company, we get soiled by walking in this world, so we need the washing of the water of the Word to cleanse us every day of our lives so we will not be stained with the cares of this world.

That he might sanctify and cleanse it with the washing of water by the word, That he might present it to himself a glorious church, not having spot, or wrinkle, or any such thing; but that it should be holy and without blemish. - Ephesians 5:26-27

We live in a church culture today of seeker friendly believers who love microwave ministries and drive through breakthroughs. They want one-hour services so they can get out of church to watch the football game. But this Foot Company is different because they love the Word of God and are bathed in it. As an apostle of the Lord Jesus Christ, I'm called to wash the feet of the Foot Company; therefore, I have written this book and pray that the words within it will wash your feet to prepare you for the calling that's upon your life. Think about the fact that Jesus even washed Judas' feet. True holiness will even wash the feet of your betrayer. If I'm going to get the boot, I'm going to get kicked with clean feet.

> *He will not suffer thy foot to be moved: he that keepeth thee will not slumber.* - Psalms 121:3

Let's look at your personal life and all that you've been through. Look at you, you are still standing! For every one of you, there's 1,000 others who would have quit. Some of you have faced physical maladies, but you're still standing. Some have experienced attacks on your marriage, but you're still standing. Many of you have had children who have suffered many challenges, but you're still standing. Others have faced financial trauma, but you are still standing. Don't cry over what's been shaken, but rejoice over what is still standing. We know the Scripture says, "All things work together for good to those who love God and are the called of God according to His purpose." The Scripture also says, "In all things we are more than conquerors through Him who loved us." Paul also declared that though our light afflictions are but for a moment, they work for us a far more exceeding and eternal weight of glory. Every affliction that comes your way is working for you! Learn to employ your problems; make them your servant so you can for fulfill your designed destiny in Christ Jesus.

> *Yea, forty years didst thou sustain them in the wilderness, so that they lacked nothing; their clothes waxed not old, and their feet swelled not.* - Nehemiah 9:21

For 40 years, God sustained the children of Israel in the wilderness. They lacked absolutely nothing; even their garments did not wear out and their feet did not swell. Though facing many challenges, this Foot Company maintains their walk by walking in love, honor, worship, integrity, and faith. God will not put you through more than what you can handle. What should have weakened you has only strengthened you for the glory of God. Let the weak say, "I'm strong!"

> *Our feet shall stand within thy gates, O Jerusalem. - Psalms 122:1-2*

The prophet Isaiah declared that His gates shall be called praise. In these coming days, the Foot Company will enter a dimension of praise higher than anything ever known to the church of Jesus Christ in the last 2,000 years. Their position is a stance of praise; it is their greatest weapon! Their praise is so powerful it will dislodge and displace demonic strongholds from atmospheres.

> *Let God arise, let his enemies be scattered: let them also that hate him flee before him. As smoke is driven away, so drive them away: as wax melteth before the fire, so let the wicked perish at the presence of God. But let the righteous be glad; let them rejoice before God: yea, let them exceedingly rejoice. - Psalm 68:1-3*

This passage will come alive! Your praises will be like: 1) the wind driving away the smoke and 2) like fire melting the wax. Look at the power of your praise in this Psalm. It declares that your prayers will make your enemies scatter, flee, and perish. Look at the digression. Perish means to vanish, give up, do away with, put to death, destroy, and to judge. As we praise Him and maintain our position of praise, we will see a digression of symptoms and problems that we face. Don't give up now! You may be one praise away from your circumstances perishing. When you mix good stewardship with praise, you will even see debt reduction. We should spend more time praising God than rebuking devils; there is a miracle in your praise. This Foot Company stands in praise, defying their circumstances. They don't just praise Him for what they see, but also for what they don't see. Don't just praise Him for the good things evident in your life, but include the things you are believing for that are not yet visible. The Scripture says that "Praise waiteth for thee, God, in Zion." When you are praising God, you signal Heaven saying, "We are waiting for You to show up and show off in our life." Praise rests upon God's Word. As faith in action, it brings God to the scene.

Thy word is a lamp unto my feet, and a light unto my path. - Psalms 119:105

Have you ever wondered why this passage tells us that His word is a lamp to our feet? Why not a lamp into our eyes? This is a passage of masked truth that is reserved for the Foot Company. This company needs revelation, the light of God's Word, to walk in more than any other generation.

Bathed in abundance of revelation, His Word is a lamp to the Foot Company.

I have refrained my feet from every evil way, that I might keep thy word. - Psalms 119:101

The Foot Company emotes a people who love truth and keep the Word of God hidden in their hearts so they can walk in all of God's ways. Their passion for the truth refrains them from the evil way. This end-time, remnant church will be known throughout eternity as the Foot Company.

Then Jesus, six days before the Passover, came to Bethany, where Lazarus was, which had been dead, whom he raised from the dead. There they made him a supper; and Martha served: but Lazarus was one of them that sat at the table with him. Then took Mary a pound of ointment of spikenard, very costly, and anointed the feet of Jesus, and wiped his feet with her hair and the house was filled with the odour of the ointment. Then saith one of his disciples, Judas Iscariot, Simon's son, which should betray him. Why was not this ointment sold for three hundred pence, and given to the poor? This he said, not that he cared for the poor; but because he was a thief, and had the bag, and bare what was put therein. Then said Jesus, Let her alone: against the day of my burying hath she kept this. For the poor always ye have with you; but me ye have not always. - John 12:1-8

This story of Mary is in all four of the Gospels. All four apostles had a different perspective of this beautiful account.

Matthew highlighted the oil poured on the head of Jesus. John's message emphasized the oil being poured on the feet. Mark focused on the oil that was in the alabaster box, and Luke underscored that oil destroys yolks of bondage. In the Gospel of John, Mary wiped the feet of Jesus with her hair. Hair in Scripture symbolizes glory. The glory of God will rest upon and cover the Foot Company.

To break this box symbolizes breaking traditions. I'm sure this box was passed down from generation to generation. The Foot Company is breaking every man-made religious tradition so they can fulfill God's assignment upon their lives in the planet. Simon (not Simon Peter) and his son, Judas, had a religious spirit and a politically correct spirit. The worship of this woman offended them both and how she poured this expensive oil out upon Jesus.
For do I now persuade men, or God? Or do I seek to please men? For if I yet pleased men, I should not be the servant of Christ. - Galatians 1:10

You will serve who or what you fear in life; if you fear man, you will serve him, but if you fear God, you will serve Him. There is a remnant in the earth today who has no fear of man but reverences God by their worship, their service, and their lives.

We will also know this Foot Company for their extravagant praise. Praise is not about pleasing people or making them feel comfortable in a worship service, but about pleasing the Lord. My wife and I have pastored our church for 25 years. There is only one person in the audience and that is the Lord Jesus Christ. He is the only person that we entertain. Our congregation knows we are not there to entertain them, but to host and celebrate the presence of God. There is a difference between a prophetic church and a performance church. At Jubilee Ministries International here in New Castle, Pennsylvania, we have chosen to be a prophetic church. We come together every week as prophetic worshipers to entertain the presence of God, not to perform our gifts and talents before the people.

Simon represents a religious spirit that wants to keep everything in a box. When religious people invite Uncle Freddie and Aunt Lucy to church, they hope you don't get too crazy that day and run around the church. When the box is broken, you find out who has a religious spirit and who doesn't. Judas told Jesus He should have sold this oil and gave it to the poor. He said this only because he was filled with greed and loved money. Jesus responded, "The poor you'll always have with you." Although giving to the poor is an important part of our ministry as the Foot Company, worshiping the Lord is greater than giving to the poor. Our church, during the pandemic, has given over $10 million of food to the poor, but our priority as kings is to worship the King. Therefore, worshiping is superior to giving to the poor, and it must be our top priority. God is seeking worshipers in this present hour and the Foot Company that is emerging will be the most radical worshipers in the church's history.

Mary's actions exposed the hearts of Judas and Simon. A Judas will hide in the house of the Lord. You will find them as part of the apostolic team, able to move in the gifts of the Spirit, heal the sick, and serve on the praise team. Judas was even Jesus' treasurer. A Judas will always want to know how the church uses its tithes and offerings. Judas' will always transition into churches during new seasons. They'll praise with you in good times, but betray you in bad times. They will never be your friend in tribulation. Please discern who is a Judah (a praiser) and who is a Judas. Judah is a giver and Judas is a taker. Love of money is the one thing that will expose a Judas. The one thing that exposes a Simon is the spirit of worship. Judas will be comfortable in the house until you start taking up special offerings. Wherever there is a Judah there will be a Judas. Judas and Simon are murmurers and complainers, critical of the church and how it operates, critical of worship and the Word preached, and always critical about how you take up an offering. Watch when worship intensifies. It will stir up the spirits of Judas and Simon in the house, right there in the pew. There are only two people other than Jesus that will be remembered in this beautiful story: Judas and Mary. Which one are you? Please choose well.

Mary broke this beautiful box as an extravagant offering. It was a fragrant oil that was poured out on Jesus. The Foot Company carries an end-time anointing to pour out on Jesus. It's beautiful that the same anointing that was poured on His head was the same that was poured upon His feet. There is a people in the earth today, the feet of Christ, who will carry the same anointing as Jesus, the head of the church. Precious and rare, this anointing will cost you because it flows out of a broken life. The same anointing that was upon Jesus' life will be the very anointing that rests on the Foot Company!

What Judas called waste, Jesus called worship. As long as the oil you have remains in the box, the box will control the flow. We have this treasure inside our earthen vessels that the excellency of this power may be of God and not of us. Religion tries to put the Holy Ghost in a box to control the flow of the Spirit. But when you break

AS LONG AS THE OIL YOU HAVE REMAINS IN THE BOX, THE BOX WILL CONTROL THE FLOW.

the box, it flows at the will of the Holy Spirit, not the will of man. Oh, how we need the Holy Ghost to flow in and through our lives freely. Some people may not be broken enough and still trying to control the Holy Spirit. It is my prayer that Jesus will break them so they can freely move in a spirit of worship and service unto the Lord.

The entrance of a Mary into your church will benefit everyone. She can rebuke your enemies without saying one word. I pray everyone reading this book will come into this powerful anointing that affects atmospheres, dictates the climate, and scatters all your enemies. In our text, Mary did not speak, but her worship rebuked all her enemies. In the coming days, worshipers will just step into rooms and everything will shift. When these emerging worshiping warriors enter a room, their arrival will benefit everyone and rebuke their enemies without saying one word. The last season boasted the excellence of words, but the new season boasts the excellence of the presence you carry, just like Mary.

I love this woman; she refused to allow anything or anyone to distract her from ministering to Jesus. Don't mess with a worshiping warrior! Jesus told them to leave her alone. Your praise and worship will rebuke and restrain all your enemies. If you praise Him, you will raise Him. You'll never know the measure of the anointing you carry until you give it away, until you pour it out. Let the pouring begin!

CHAPTER 13

Leaping Into Destiny

And it came to pass, after the year was expired, at the time when kings go forth to battle, that David sent Joab, and his servants with him, and all Israel; and they destroyed the children of Ammon and besieged Rabbah. But David tarried still at Jerusalem. - 2 Samuel 11:1

As we have already stated, the Bible is about a King, His Kingdom, and His royal family. Jesus came to set up a Kingdom, not a religion, and to fill His Kingdom with royal kings.

In the days of David, the kings would go together to battle every spring, but one year David stayed home and took a sabbatical. When David should have been on the battlefield, he found himself in the bedroom with a woman named Bathsheba. Man was created for Kingdom conquest and adventure. When the Kingdom stands as only a Sunday event, man's passionate need for conquest is misplaced. When men and women in the marketplace do not have a clear vision regarding their calling in the seven spheres of society, their conquest and adventure will be misdirected. Misplaced conquest and adventure will lead men into unproductive lifestyles. When King David forfeited his place on the battlefield, he found himself in the bedroom; this is misplaced conquest. Today's true battlefield for kings is in the marketplace, or what we call the seven mountains of society that include family, church, media, government, education, arts/entertainment, and finance/business.

And it shall come to pass in the last days, that the mountain of the Lord's house shall be established in the top of the mountains, and shall be exalted above the hills; and all nations shall flow unto it. - Isaiah 2:2

As a 21st-century church, we commission kings into the marketplace as change agents so they can fulfill their calling in Christ by recovering and restoring the earth for King Jesus and bringing it under His Kingdom rule.

For the Son of man is come to seek and to save that which was lost. - Luke 19:10

The Lord spoke through the Prophet Amos that we are not to be at ease in Zion. In modern vernacular, he warned us it is dangerous when we want an easy life. There is an assembly of kings emerging who are going to occupy every sphere of society until Jesus comes.

> *And he called his ten servants, and delivered them ten pounds, and said unto them, Occupy till I come. - Luke 19:13*

This word occupy is being used in a parable in which a wealthy nobleman gave his servants a certain amount of money and told them to occupy until he returned. Two of his servants multiplied what they had been given and were granted authority over cities. This word occupy is a military word that was used to seize territory. Likewise we are to invade and occupy every sphere of society and influence it with the gospel of the Kingdom until Jesus returns to planet earth. The planet does not belong to the devil, but to Mr. and Mrs. Jesus Christ, Jesus the Bridegroom and His bride, the church.

THERE IS AN ASSEMBLY OF KINGS EMERGING WHO ARE GOING TO OCCUPY EVERY SPHERE OF SOCIETY UNTIL JESUS COMES.

You can't become a king when you're in a church filled

with only priests and prophets. There must be a divine interaction and synergy with other kings. Kings serve much better when they serve with other kings.

> *Iron sharpeneth iron; so a man sharpeneth the countenance of his friend. - Proverbs 27:17*

Everything about these emerging kings is non-competitive. We draw from each other's gift clusters as we advance the Kingdom in the earth and celebrate one another's gifts, callings and anointings. These kings that are emerging in the earth today change the earth by releasing what's in Heaven. They will put a demand on Heaven to release the glory and riches of the Kingdom by the atmospheres they create, the prayers they pray, the words they speak and the faith-filled decrees that go forth from their mouths. God is restricted on the earth to move without man's consent; He needs our permission.

> *"I tell you the truth, whatever you forbid on earth will be forbidden in heaven, and whatever you permit on earth will be permitted in heaven. - Matthew 18:18 NLT.*

I've always been impressed by all the miracles that Jesus performed. He walked on water, cleansed the lepers, turned water into wine, raised the dead, opened blind eyes and the list was endless. What I find unusual is that I never see in Scripture where the disciples asked Him how He did these amazing miracles. The only thing they asked was, "Teach us to pray." They did not ask for six steps on how to open blind eyes and raise the dead, but asked, "Teach us to pray, Lord." These emerging kings desired to learn how to pray from the King of kings. The secret of Jesus' success was a life of prayer. So it is with every king that's emerging in the earth today. Jesus spent more time in private prayer than He did a life in public; His private life was the secret to His success. His primary ministry was to His Heavenly Father and not to man. His priestly ministry to the Father was the catalyst for His kingly ministry and doing miracles on the earth.

As we stated in a previous chapter, God cannot intervene in the earth without mankind giving Him permission. When He said, "Let them have dominion," it became a law. Amos said, "How can two walk together except they agree?" God restricts Himself to acting in the boundaries of His covenant. This explains many questions as to why God did not intervene in some evil occurrences that have taken place in the earth. God cannot walk in the earth unless someone cooperates with Him. Our prayers act as the exercise of our covenant with God, and our words must prophetically agree with King Jesus and His Word. Our prayers give God the green light to invade the earth. There is nowhere in Scripture where God does anything without mankind's participation. When we pray, God works!

And in the morning, rising a great while before day, he

went out, and departed into a solitary place, and there prayed. - Mark 1:35

Jesus would spend His early waking hours communing with and praying to His Heavenly Father, but it only took Him seconds to heal the sick and raise the dead. Jesus rose early to pray in the morning, but in the evening He would deliver and heal creation.

And at even when the sun did set, they brought unto him all that were diseased, and them that were possessed with devils. And all the city was gathered together at the door. And he healed many that were sick of divers diseases and cast out many devils; and suffered not the devils to speak, because they knew him. - Mark 1:32-34

We see an amazing example of this principle in Matthew 17 when Jesus takes Peter, James, and John up into the Mountain of Transfiguration, where they were marinating in the presence of God. At the bottom of the mountain were nine of Jesus' disciples, trying to deliver a young boy who had seizures. Like many Christians today who try to get people healed and delivered but to no avail, likewise, these nine disciples could not cure this boy.

I am the vine, ye are the branches: He that abideth in me, and I in him, the same bringeth forth much fruit: for without me ye can do nothing. - John 15:5

The absence of God's presence made their power inoperative. It's important that today's emerging kings are a presence driven people. Our priestly calling is to minister to God so He can empower us in our kingly calling to heal and deliver creation. Once we minister to God, then and only then do we qualify to minister to man. There must be up-reach before there's outreach. Jesus came down the mountain, rebuked the devil and healed the boy instantly. Why couldn't the nine cast the devil out of this boy? Jesus said this kind goes out by prayer and fasting. Not rebuking, not shouting, not screaming, but by prayer and fasting and not even by using His Name, but by prayer and fasting. If you spend one hour with the Lord in the morning, you will solve most of your problems quickly throughout the day.

Two of Jesus' disciples followed His example and we see this in the beautiful story with Peter and John in the book of Acts.

> *Now Peter and John went up together into the temple at the hour of prayer, being the ninth hour. And a certain man lame from his mother's womb was carried, whom they laid daily at the gate of the temple which is called Beautiful, to ask alms of them that entered into the temple; Who seeing Peter and John about to go into the temple asked an alms. And Peter, fastening his eyes upon him with John, said, look on us. And he gave heed unto them, expecting to receive something of them. Then Peter said, silver and gold have I none; but such as I have give I thee: In the name of Jesus Christ of Nazareth rise up and walk. And he took him by the right hand, and lifted him up and immediately his*

feet and ankle bones received strength. And he leaping up stood, and walked, and entered with them into the temple, walking, and leaping, and praising God. And all the people saw him walking and praising God: And they knew that it was he which sat for alms at the Beautiful gate of the temple: and they were filled with wonder and amazement at that which had happened unto him.
- Acts 3:1-10

Our story begins with Peter and John going up together to the temple to pray, being the ninth hour. The ninth hour was the time the priests were offering incense to the Lord, a type of prayer and intercession. There they met a man who was lame from his mother's womb and carried daily to the temple, which was at a gate they called Beautiful. The word beautiful in the Greek is the word which means a certain season, a fixed time and a definite time. There are certain seasons in which God endues and clothes His chosen saints with His power; we are coming into one of those seasons. This is the first miracle recorded after Pentecost took place. The principle of first mention in Scripture sets a standard, establishing a precedence and pattern.

This man was born with a condition that restricted him from walking. When you were born, you had no choice in the matter. You did not choose when you were born, to whom you were born to or where you were born. You were born at an appointed time, a set time, and nothing was accidental about your birth; nothing was illegitimate about your birth. At Texas A&M University's statistical department, they calculated the odds of a specific individual being born. To accomplish this, they calculated the number of genetic possibilities that contribute to a birth, the number of hours per month of female fertility and a long list of more considerations. The bottom line was that the chance of you being born was one in 1.3×10 to the 29th power. 1 in 130,000,000,000,000,000,000,000,000,000 was your odds of being here. Yes, you were wonderfully and fearfully made, and you are incredibly called and chosen for such a time as this!

Every idea has a time in which it's meant to be birthed. And long before you were ever conceived in your mama's womb, you were an idea in the mind of God.

Then said I, Lo, I come: in the volume of the book it is written of me... - Psalms 40:7

God looked and saw you in the volume of the book and said that you are uncommonly outrageous and beautiful. Yes, in the eyes of Heaven, you're one of a kind, a masterpiece. You never fit into the world, you couldn't get comfortable in religion, and some of you did not even fit in with your own family. You are a square peg in a round hole. The Kingdom was not your choice; it was God's choice. He apprehended you and set you in His Kingdom. Like a rare diamond in a ring, so are you sovereignly set in the Kingdom for this moment in history. Every idea and dream and every vision you have has a sovereign time to be born. You are uniquely and wonderfully prepared to fulfill God's dream for your life. You are God's dream come true!

What time is it? It's time to leap into destiny. The Bible is filled with divine leaps. Our story in Acts chapter 3 is one of those divine moments. The Bible calls this man "a certain man," not just any man. Lame from his mother's womb, he was carried to this gate called Beautiful. Every day, he was carried and let down at this gate, the entrance of the temple. God's holy prophets release prophetic words for your purpose and destiny. Similarly, they carry you to the gate where you can see through to the dream, the destiny, and the vision God has for your life. These powerful prophecies carry you to the threshold of your destiny. This man could see through the gate but could not walk through it. Although we have ugly situations in the stories of our lives, we have a gate that is called Beautiful. I want to prophesy over every one of your ugly circumstances, whether they be financial, physical, or any discouraging report you may have received. I prophesy that every lame experience is about to be behind you and you're getting ready to walk through this gate called Beautiful.

I know thy works: behold; I have set before thee an open door, and no man can shut it: for thou hast a little strength, and hast kept my word, and hast not denied my name. - Revelation 3:8

There is an open door before us, the word door in the Greek

means: a way or a passage. Get ready, there is an open door that no man can shut or keep you out of!

For a great door and effectual is opened unto me, and there are many adversaries. - 1 Corinthians 16:9

An open door in Scripture means the entrance into a new place in God. There is an open door of unprecedented opportunities. Opposition is the hinges on which the door of opportunity swings wide open. This is not a door with a doorknob and you don't even need keys; it's just a wide, open door and no one can shut it. This open door is God's yes and amen: yes, you can have that miracle, yes, you can receive your healing, yes, you can walk in your ministry, and yes, you can receive that blessing and your breakthrough.

For all the promises of God in him are yea, and in him Amen, unto the glory of God by us. - 2 Corinthians 1:20

The religious order let this lame man in Acts down every day. Maybe you've been let down by religion, or by friends and family members. The Levitical priest of that day could only carry him to the gate, but failed to deliver him and raise him up out of his affliction. The Levitical priesthood were priests only and not kings; therefore, they could have compassion upon this man as priests, but could not deliver this man as kings could. It would take a new priesthood after the order of Melchizedek, who were both priests and kings. Peter and John represent this new priesthood of priests and kings; not only would they have compassion for this man, but they also had the authority to raise him up. Without the kingly anointing, the priesthood had no authority, thus inhibiting their rule and reign over the circumstances of the people. As priests, we minister to the Lord in prayer and worship, and as kings, we minister and deliver creation from their lame condition.

Nothing happened until Peter and John showed up. Likewise, some things will not happen until you show up. Peter said, "Look on us," which literally means "Look into us." Christ, the hope of glory, is in you and me. Miracles happen when we see the Christ in others.

There are two kinds of people who need to be carried: the handicapped and babies. Many churches are just nurseries and hospitals for immature people and those who have been hurt. So we need the kings to arise to deliver them from their present condition. I have learned in over 30 years of ministry that many believers want leaders to lower their standards to come down to their level, but Peter and John did not come down to this man's level. Instead, they reached down and there is a big difference. They could have been simply sympathetic, but they chose to empower this man. This book was not meant to come down where you are, but to reach down and to lift you up so you can leap into destiny. Real kings do not come down to where you are but reach down to lift you up into your designed destiny.

I've seen so many people leave church because they would rather be carried than walk themselves. God has called us to be childlike, but not to be childish. To be childlike is to have no fear, no doubts, a pure trust in God, to be willing and passionate. Once again, there are only two kinds of people that you carry, lame folk and babies. One needs to be healed, the other needs to grow up, but both are called to walk in the Kingdom.

GOD HAS CALLED US TO BE CHILDLIKE, BUT NOT TO BE CHILDISH.

When Peter and John, representatives of this new priesthood, showed up, everything changed. The world that we are presently in is about to dramatically change as this new breed of kings arises. Before we leap into destiny, we must first emphasize learning to walk. This man walked before he leaped. We can't leap into our destiny if we walk in the flesh, pride, condemnation, fear, doubt, bitterness, and unforgiveness. We must walk by faith, walk in the Spirit, walk in love, walk as children of light, walk in wisdom, walk in honesty, and walk in truth.

He that saith he abideth in him ought himself also so to walk, even as he walked. - 1 John 2:6

John the Apostle said we are to walk as Jesus did. Please make sure that you walk with the right people because you cannot get into your destiny on your own. You can't enter your destiny, your spiritual inheritance, or the promises of God alone; you must be in the right company following the right leaders. Just being saved and filled with the Holy Ghost doesn't promise that you will fulfill your destiny in Christ. You need to be with a company of other kings, who can strengthen your walk like Peter and John, so you can leap into your destiny. Everyone needs a Peter and John to fulfill their destiny. What will it take for you to enter your destiny? Peter represents revelation and John represents intimacy. Intimacy with your Heavenly Father and a revelation of your priestly, kingly, and prophetic anointing will prepare you for your destiny.

Religion will let you down, but real, five-fold leaders will lift you up as a king to rule and reign with Christ over all your circumstances. This is an apostolic season where we rule as kings in this life. Most believers are ruled by life instead of ruling in life. A couple of years ago, a national survey was done and revealed that 98% of all believers had no revelatory understanding of the Kingdom and their authority to rule and reign in life. Why? Religion prepares people for Heaven, but not to rule in this life. That's why apostles are emerging in the earth today who carry a revelation of our true identity and authority in Christ.

This man, while laying at the gate called Beautiful, received a suddenly. God's about to release some 11th hour suddenlies to the body of Christ. And you'll instantly go from a lame to a leap! Many will walk in the Kingdom of God immediately. Unexpected and unannounced, you could be sick one day and suddenly healed, broke one day and the next day the bills are paid, suddenly debt-free, kids running from God one day and suddenly they come to church the next day.

We now stand at the threshold of our destiny. Together, we will leap into destiny for the glory of God. Many saints are presently at a gate called Beautiful, and their ugly situation is about to become beautiful. God is about to reveal to you that He is beautiful in every situation. The most beautiful time of your life is right before you. We are at a gate called Beautiful; Beautiful means to be at the right hour and at the right season. This is a set time to favor the remnant church of Jesus Christ.

Thou shalt arise, and have mercy upon Zion: for the time to favour her, yea, the set time, is come. - Psalms 102:13

We're entering a season of suddenlies. You are just before a suddenly!

I have declared the former things from the beginning; and they went forth out of my mouth, and I shewed

> *them; I did them suddenly, and they came to pass. - Isaiah 48:3*

Every suddenly that you'll ever have has already happened. God has no subsequent thoughts, no afterthoughts; He is God, and He changes not. You're not an afterthought; you were a premeditated thought in the mind of God before angels were ever created.

> *Behold, I will send my messenger, and he shall prepare the way before me: and the Lord, whom ye seek, shall suddenly come to his temple, even the messenger of the covenant, whom ye delight in: behold, he shall come, saith the Lord of hosts. - Malachi 3:1*

The prophet said, "the Lord whom you seek shall suddenly come to His temple." Suddenlies are attracted to you because you are the temple of God. But please remember suddenlies do not come to sleepers, but to the seekers! No suddenly should surprise you. You've been preparing your whole life for suddenlies. The Lord premeditated every suddenly you'll ever have. Whatever is happening in your time, space, and world usually contradicts what God is about to do. In fact, crisis is the environment for your suddenly. Ugly situations scream out that suddenlies are on their way! To the natural mind and with circumstantial evidence, it looks like nothing may be happening in your time, space, world, but in the supernatural mind, the Heavens are full of suddenlies. Heaven is alive and pregnant with these suddenlies and angels are standing at attention, ready to release your suddenly. Yes, anything can happen now!

> *And suddenly there was with the angel a multitude of the heavenly host praising God, and saying, Glory to God in the highest, and on earth peace, good will toward men. - Luke 2:13,14*

There was 400 years of silence in the world right before Christ's birth. No prophetic words were spoken during this time and all the earth was in a spiritual slumber. Darkness covered the earth but suddenly, the glory of the Lord appeared. Yes, suddenly a host of heavenly angels appeared and began to praise God saying, "Glory to God in the highest, peace on earth goodwill toward men." Every suddenly is heralded by praise. Praise is the environment for your suddenly. That's why we send Judah (i.e. praise) first. There will always be silence before a suddenly. Many times, when we go through a difficult season, we have the temptation to quit. I urge you to limp forward if you must until you can leap into the destiny God designed for you. Don't quit, don't walk away, but keep believing, keep

PRAISE IS THE ENVIRONMENT FOR YOUR SUDDENLY.

praising, and keep moving. You may be just one step away from your suddenly.

Many of you have been dropped by a mother or a father, a friend, a teacher, a man or a woman, or maybe a preacher has let you down. Don't quit now, keep limping until you leap; if you have to crawl, then crawl. Those who lamed you cannot stop your leap from happening. So many saints have been rejected, hurt, broken, forgotten, and let down, but keep pressing forward because you're going to limp your way into a leap. Sick in your body? Don't quit! Can't pay the bills? Don't quit! Kids acting crazy? Don't quit! Weary in well doing? Don't quit! Come hell or high water, you're getting ready to leap into something new. Like David, who ran through a troop and leaped over a wall, you're getting ready to leap over some walls and over whatever barriers and obstacles stand in your way. Get ready to leap!

At the time of writing this book, my son just graduated from high school. He was the point guard for his senior high basketball team. My son has an incredible gift and has worked very hard for the past 12 years to develop the gift the Lord gave him to play basketball. I had the incredible privilege of coaching my son's team. However, with Covid restrictions, they almost did not have a season. In addition, he had a team full of less skilled players than their opposing teams. The odds were against us. Halfway through the year, it looked like we would not even make it to the playoffs, let alone making it to the championship game. Somehow, we found our way into the playoffs; my son stepped up his game, and the team followed his lead. His passion and pursuit became contagious, and they won both playoff games qualifying for the championship. The team we were playing in the championship game would be a challenge, since they had already beaten us twice during the regular season. But my son, Christian Mark, stepped up to the challenge! Even though our team had a "limp" at the beginning of the season, they were about to leap into their destiny. With 25 points, he led his team to an incredible victorious upset, and they won the championship against all odds! These underdogs went from a lame to a leap!

You can't throw in the towel. There will be no towel throwing in this game; take your towel back! If you have to limp, limp by faith and get ready to leap. You will outlive your limp, for your legs are about to receive strength. You've come too far to quit now and walk away. Don't give up now! You might be only one moment away from leaping through that Gate called Beautiful. God is in the lifting up mood today. Let Him lift up your countenance and always remember He's the Glory and the Lifter of your head. He can lift the beggar from the dunghill. When the enemy comes in like a flood, He will lift you up as a standard. Get ready, kings of the Most High God, to leap into destiny! May the real kings arise!

DR. MARK KAUFFMAN

ABOUT DR. MARK E. KAUFFMAN

Being passionately involved in both business and ministry, Dr. Mark Kauffman possesses a unique ability to equip and train marketplace leaders to link the idea of prosperity to a God-given plan that will advance the Kingdom of God in the earth. His heart is to see the body of Christ demonstrate the nature and ministry of the Lord Jesus, thus fulfilling their designed destiny.

He is the founder and overseeing Apostle of Jubilee Ministries International City Church located in New Castle, Pennsylvania. His ministry expands over 30 years. Through the word of knowledge and the gifts of healing and prophecy, he sees many miracles as he ministers the Gospel of the Kingdom. Dr. Kauffman received his Doctorate of Divinity from Tabernacle Bible School and University.

Since 1987, Dr. Kauffman has successfully owned and operated Butz Flowers Gifts and Home Décor, the second oldest florist in the United States and ranked in the top 500 of 30,000 florists in the world. He is the Chief Executive Officer of Global Investments, Global Impact Mega Corporation, and Destiny Developers.

Dr. Kauffman also oversees The International Network of Kingdom Leaders (INK), a worldwide network of five-fold leaders, churches, and businesses. In addition, he serves as the CEO of the Christian Chamber of Commerce of Western Pennsylvania (CCCWP), an empowerment agency to equip, train and prepare marketplace leaders to influence, transform and lead the 21st century Kingdom reformation.

Dr. Kauffman also serves as CEO of Kingdom Broadcasting Network (KBN), which was established in 2014 to recover Christian values and virtues by giving them expression through various media outlets. In 2021, Dr. Kauffman along with his wife Dr. Jill Kauffman created and now host The Apostolic Voice, a 30-minute program which currently airs Sundays from 8:00 p.m. to 8:30 p.m. EST, and Mondays from 12:00 p.m. to 12:30 p.m. on Dominion TV.

The cry in this present hour is for Godly leadership. Dr. Kauffman has authored *The Presence Driven Leader*, which is a book filled with 700 quotes that are a clarion call to awaken the Presence driven leader in every reader and quicken them to the purpose and plan for God in their life.

For over 30 years, Mark has been happily married to Dr. Jill Kauffman, who works tirelessly alongside him to see the Kingdom of God advance, therefore, impacting generations. They have three sons, Christian Mark, Anthony, and Ryan, and three grandchildren.

Additional Resources by Dr. Mark Kauffman

THE PRESENCE DRIVEN LEADER

DRMARKKAUFFMAN.ORG

WHAT KIND OF A LEADER ARE YOU?

God is raising up a new company of leaders who will lead people into fresh encounters with His presence – greater encounters than they have ever before experienced. Today's leaders must not be position driven. Even purpose driven leaders run the risk of serving their own pursuits unless they are focused on true purpose in the Kingdom – intimacy with the Father.

When leaders become presence driven, they fulfill true destiny – to reveal God to their generation (Psalm 71:18).

A proven leader in both business and ministry, Dr. Mark Kauffman has dedicated his life to the passionate pursuit of God's presence. The Presence Driven Leader is a compilation of fundamental leadership principles viewed through this unique filter. This book will empower you with nearly 700 powerful, memorable leadership quotes.

www.ingramcontent.com/pod-product-compliance
Lightning Source LLC
Chambersburg PA
CBHW060351190426
43201CB00044B/2020